MUSSOORIE

TALES FROM THE HILLS

MONTAGE

DIVYAROOP BHATNAGAR

Om Books International

Reprinted in 2026

Om Books International

Corporate & Editorial Office
A-12, Sector 64, Noida 201 301
Uttar Pradesh, India
Phone: +91 120 477 4100
Email: editorial@ombooks.com
Website: www.ombooksinternational.com

Sales Office
107, Ansari Road, Darya Ganj,
New Delhi 110 002, India
Phone: +91 11 4000 9000
Email: sales@ombooks.com
Website: www.ombooks.com

ISBN: 978-93-6395-474-8

Printed in India

10 9 8 7 6 5 4 3 2

Dedication

To my grandparents, Dr K.P. Bhatnagar and Sumati Devi Bhatnagar. It was they who instilled in us the love for Mussoorie when we were children.

To that magical mountain refuge which has always been such a large part of my life.

Our love for Mussoorie has endured through the years, and my grandparents would surely be happy to see our grandchildren enjoying the place as much today as they themselves did a hundred years ago.

Divyaroop (Debu) Bhatnagar was born and brought up in Kanpur. As a child, his family would go to Mussoorie in summer for the children's school vacations and the love for the place and the mountains have stayed with him for a lifetime. Debu studied at IIT Kanpur and IIM Calcutta and had a long career with consumer products companies in India and abroad as a CEO and an MD. Along with a few close friends and colleagues, he later set up a consulting company.

Debu loves reading, travelling, golf and bridge. He has been writing from 2018 when his first book, *Journey to the Hills and Other Stories* was published. His next book, *The Mussoorie Murders* was published by Om Books International in 2023. It has gone on to become a national bestseller, with three reprints coming in quick succession.

He has two grown-up daughters and three lovely granddaughters, and lives in Gurgaon with his wife, Devi.

Debu can be contacted at authordebu@gmail.com

Contents

1

Mountain Rest

The lace curtains were usually drawn. In the few instances when the window was slightly opened to let in some fresh air, the curtains moved a little in the gentle breeze as if sensing a moment of freedom. The little house stood primly at Camel's Back Road. It was accessible by a small staircase bordered by flowerpots in which blue and pink hydrangeas grew, in a carefully trimmed pattern. The tiny lawn adjoining the house had a garden table, accompanied with a red-and-white umbrella and two chairs. But nobody had ever seen anyone sitting there. The windows were painted white, shining brightly in contrast to the brick walls and red tin roof.

There was a little wooden nameplate mounted on the wall next to the white-painted wicket gate at the foot of the stairs. It read 'Mountain Rest' and announced the owner's name as Kamal Kapoor. The house made a determined attempt to look bright and cheerful and to some extent succeeded when the sun shone. As the sun set, it had a more withdrawn and cloistered look. Lights glowed at dusk from behind the lace curtains, but they were soon extinguished as darkness fell and the house withdrew into its self-imposed solitude.

A dour older woman, grey-haired and slightly bent, looked after the house. She was not from Mussoorie and did not talk to any of the local people. No one came to cook or clean, so she obviously did all the work herself. She went shopping at the Mall Road every other day and her movements and preferences were keenly observed and commented upon.

"I wonder if she lives alone in that house. She hardly buys anything."

"She buys expensive things—shampoos and creams—but surely not for herself!"

"Never buys a newspaper or a magazine. Maybe she can't read, that's why."

The woman may have heard the voices around her, but she never commented, never looked anyone in the eye, never smiled or frowned, and just went for a brief walk carrying her shopping bag and returned as soon as she had completed her task. She wore a drab sari and a shawl wrapped around her. The only addition when winter set in and it was bitterly cold was a woollen coat with a hood over her sari. Otherwise, her routine never varied.

Whenever she would leave, she would lock the front door of the house very carefully with a big iron padlock, stowing away the key in her brown leather purse, which in turn was kept in the shopping bag.

"See, she locks the house when she leaves for the market. Surely that means that there is no one else inside."

The voices were indefatigable, layers and layers of curiosity, delving into minute details, but no one had the courage to confront the woman or talk to her.

On the first Sunday of May every year, regular as clockwork, a man came to the house. He always arrived after dark, so no one could be completely sure of what he looked like or how old he was. He was a tall, thin person dressed in a tweed coat with a tie. He would walk in, opening the wicket gate, which would be left unlocked knowing about his arrival. He would then knock softly on the front door. It opened with a slither of light and the woman's silhouette was briefly visible before the door closed behind them.

The man always stayed for two weeks. When he was there, the windows would be thrown open and the lace curtains swayed in the breeze. He stayed indoors during the day but sat outside on the tiny lawn as dusk descended. During his stay, the woman would buy more things from the market, and for a time, the house would seem almost cheerful again.

"I wonder who he is? He seems too young to be that woman's husband."

"He's too well dressed. She must be his servant."

"Why does he come here? Maybe the woman is his mistress."

"That can't be. She's too old!"

"Stranger things have been known to happen!"

"Is he the owner? Is there another woman in the house? This one's too ugly!"

The voices were relentless, gossipy and malicious. They churned round and round, year after year, as the man came and went. With time, the woman's posture stooped a little and her hair turned greyer than before, but that was it, for nothing else changed. The voices continued with renewed vigour as younger ones joined in, but the lot of them remained as ignorant as ever.

The old woman would go to Charles Chemist shop near Picture Palace once a month. The chemist's assistant would always have a packet ready for her, which she paid for quickly and left. Only once in April when the snow had melted but there was a cold fresh breeze and sparkling skies, there was no packet awaiting her.

The voices overheard her strained, anxious questions. The assistant answered as best as he could, then the owner came and spoke. "Supplies have not come in from Delhi. It happens sometimes," he said soothingly.

"By when then?" she asked almost tearfully.

"I can't say. But I will telephone them to inquire," said the owner reassuringly.

With that she had to be content. Dragging her feet, she walked back slowly. Then—in what was a break from her routine—she climbed up the slope at Kulri and walked down towards *jhulaghar*, the children's park, where she sat on a bench overlooking the Doon Valley. She sat there for a long while looking at the mist and haze on the sunlit valley with unseeing eyes. Then she got up and walked down Lavender Lane on the way to her house.

After that day, the woman went to Charles Chemist shop every day. Her anxious inquiries were met with a refusal every time until, at last, after a fortnight the owner came out and handed her a packet himself.

"This just arrived," he said. "I have asked them to send supplies for two months, so that we will not have this problem again."

"That's very kind of you," said the woman, unexpectedly in English, accepting the packet. After paying the owner, she paused to say a few words of gratitude and good wishes.

The voices heard her speak in her normal tone for the first time.

"She sounds educated."

"She speaks English fluently. She's no servant. And that's for sure."

"Wonder whom she's buying medicines for?"

"Maybe for herself."

The voices spoke of the woman with a new respect. In their world, the woman's speech was as important as it had been for Eliza Doolittle. If anything, they were more intrigued than ever. If the woman was educated, was she the mistress of the house? Did she live alone? Who was the man who came to visit her? They watched her and listened and gossiped. It was the same as usual.

In August the same year, there was a great hullabaloo. The woman came out of the house in the morning before her usual time and instead of walking towards her usual shops, she turned towards the White Palisades Hotel. Without stopping to catch a breath, she climbed straight up Gun Hill and went inside St Catherine's Hospital. Very soon, Dr Prasad, accompanied by a nurse, came out of the hospital and started striding towards the house. They were inside for a long time. The voices watched this new turn of events and broke out in a fresh deluge of whispers.

"There is obviously someone else inside."

"Someone who is ill." Sage nods accompanied this profound statement.

The doctor and nurse came out of the house, looking grim and saddened. They did not look at anyone or talk to the voices surrounding them who eagerly awaited news of any sort. As night fell, the house shut down as usual, but a light burned inside through the night.

As the sun rose over Lal Tibba, a new day dawned. The man who used to visit first Sunday of May every year came by late morning and so did an undertaker. Soon, a body wrapped in white cloth from head to toe was spotted being taken out. Nobody could make out whether it was that of a man, woman, or child. A horse cart was summoned and the small cortege comprising the man and woman passed down Camel's Back Road. At last, one of the voices found the courage to speak.

"We are sorry for your loss," she said, addressing the woman.

She nodded, her eyes red and tearless. Suddenly, she spoke, "She was my daughter, my beloved child. And now she has gone." Her voice broke and cracked but still no tears came.

"What happened to her?"

"She was ill for a long time. She contracted leprosy just after we got married," said the man in a broken voice.

The voices recoiled, afraid of contagion, but still the bravest of them spoke again, "Is that why you kept her hidden here?"

"Yes, it was incurable, but it could be contained. She had to have her medicine daily. But finally, her ravaged body could take no more." The man was crying openly while the woman stood stoically beside him.

The voices were stilled, shocked into silence.

2

Marilyn Villa

It is a steep climb up from the White Palisades Hotel on the Mall Road to Gun Hill. As you reach the top, the road forks. On the right, on the northern face of Gun Hill the road descends and ascends again leaving St Catherine's Hospital behind. The views of both Doon Valley and the snow-capped peaks are equally spectacular from here. A steep slope leads up to Marilyn Villa, circles it and goes to the houses behind. The house has two entrances. A broad gravel path led to an outhouse and the back of the house. Just beyond, after a little curve in the road, there was a wide, shallow brickwork staircase that led to a veranda. The staircase was bordered by ornamental flowerpots in which hydrangeas grew. They were not well tended and even the terrace garden looked unkempt with a few dahlias and gladioli that seemed to bloom despite the indifference of the owners of the house.

The house was built on two levels, with an enclosed veranda on the first floor. It has a beautiful view of Bandarpunch, and the Nanda Devi ranges towards the right. An idyllic location. Perched up in the clouds, it is still just a short walk down to the Mall Road and to

Camel's Back Road on the other side near the graveyard. Surprising, therefore, that Marilyn Villa had remained empty for years, slowly going to seed after the British owners left in the 1940s.

It was in 1963 that a man came inquiring about the house. An old chowkidar and his wife lived in the outhouse and had lived there for a long time. Many of the glass panes in their house had broken over the years and they had replaced them with sheets from old Dalda tins, so that the place looked like an advertisement for *vanaspati,* the hydrogenated vegetable oil. Having not received any visitors for years, they were somewhat bemused to see the man who stood outside their door.

"Namaste, saheb," said the chowkidar, deciding to attend to the man after hearing the constant knocks.

"Namaste, bhaiya. Whose house is this?" the man asked. He was dressed in cotton trousers and a thick pullover to keep out the cold breeze. It was an unusually cold year, and it was still early in the season.

"I don't know, saheb," said the chowkidar.

"How is that? You are living here, so surely you must be knowing who owns the house," the man queried.

"I have been the chowkidar of this house since British times, saheb. The owner was a gora saheb who left the country before Independence," replied the chowkidar.

"He must have sold the house to someone," the man wondered aloud.

"I don't know, saheb. We have been staying here since the time he was the owner. When he left, he gave us some money but did not tell us anything. We just kept on staying here, but he never came back," said the chowkidar.

"Did he ever write to you?" The man seemed intrigued by the story.

"No, saheb. Anyway, we can't read." He seemed reluctant to prolong the conversation and started walking towards the outhouse.

The man nodded and took his leave. It was evident that the chowkidar either did not know much about the house or was holding himself back for some unknown reason. Arun Saran, for that was the man's name, had liked the house on sight. He was a rich businessman from Bombay who had wound down his work after his wife's mental health had started deteriorating. He now wanted to spend the rest of his years with her in a quiet place where she could recoup her mental balance, if it was at all possible. He had spent time in Mussoorie as a child and it seemed to be the natural place for them to come to as a refuge. He had liked Marilyn Villa very much as it was surrounded with magnificent views. It was also close to St Catherine's Hospital, in case his wife needed help at any point of time. He resolved to find out about the owners.

Arun walked into the tiny office of Prithvi Chand Bajaj, the real estate agent, just next to the First Bank of India, the very next day.

"Do you have any good houses for sale?" Arun asked, coming straight to the point.

"We have a few. What sort of house are you looking for, sir?" Mr Bajaj asked.

"I want a house in a quiet place, though not very far away from the bazaar," said Arun.

The agent took out some files and started discussing with Arun. After a while, Arun asked abruptly, "Is Marilyn Villa for sale?"

The estate agent paused. "Marilyn Villa? You mean the dilapidated house high on Gun Hill?" he asked in an astonished voice. "Why would you want to buy that house? There are many others available that are in much better shape."

"I saw the place yesterday and I liked it a lot," said Arun straightforwardly.

"I can try and find out, sir," said the estate agent. "Please give me a little time."

Arun went back to the estate agent after a few days.

"I have some good news for you," said the agent. "I spoke to my father about what we had discussed and he remembered that we had received a letter from a lawyer in London about Marilyn Villa a few years ago. I managed to find the letter and I have it here with me."

Arun took the typed letter from the agent. It basically said that the owner of Marilyn Villa, George Mackintosh, had passed away and that his heirs wanted to sell the property. The lawyer was representing them, and he had written to Mr Bajaj in Mussoorie to help him find a buyer.

"Well, that's great news! I'm delighted," exclaimed Arun.

"Yes, it's quite a coincidence," said Mr Bajaj smiling.

"Though it is surprising that the house has not been sold since you received the letter," said Arun casually.

He had bent down to stir the tea that had just arrived and thus missed the sudden change of expression on Mr Bajaj's face.

"Please go ahead and correspond with the lawyer on my behalf," said Arun. There was a brief discussion about the terms and conditions before they parted. Arun went back to the White Palisades Hotel where he was staying and left the next day for Bombay.

Arun heard from Mr Bajaj almost three months later. The London lawyer had agreed to his offer, that too without much discussion. Now that all the background work was complete, Mr Bajaj wanted Arun to come to Mussoorie for registering the property and completing the transaction. He soon travelled to Mussoorie and by October the house was his.

"Do you know a good contractor who can work on the house?" Arun asked. They were sitting in Mr Bajaj's office having tea after returning from their visit at Mussoorie Municipality for the registration work.

"I think Mr Semwal will be the right man for you. I will ask him to meet you at your hotel today."

Arun met Mr Semwal later that day and walked up to Marilyn Villa with him. The chowkidar had heard the news that the house had been sold and was understandably worried about his future. Arun reassured him and asked him to open the door. They entered the house from the backdoor.

They were the first people to step foot inside the house in several years. The drawing room was festooned in cobwebs. The chandelier and decaying furniture were covered with moth-eaten cloth and the whole place smelled of must and gloom.

"Oh my! This place looks awful!" Arun exclaimed.

"That can be easily cleaned up, sir," Mr Semwal was quick to add. He was going around tapping the walls and floor. He checked the ceiling using a stick. "The good thing is that the structure is still sound. Repairing that would have meant major work. If you agree, I will send some men to clean up the place so that we can walk around and then decide what work is to be done."

"That sounds good." said Arun.

They once again met at Marilyn Villa a few days later. The house was looking much cleaner this time. All the cobwebs had disappeared. The floor had been swept and swabbed, and the cloth covers had been thrown away. The sofas in the drawing room were sagging but serviceable. There was a dining room on the left with the kitchen beyond that. On the left was a staircase, leading to a bedroom on the upper floor. Arun's interest was piqued by the other staircase leading to the basement.

"There is an underground storeroom, full of all sorts of things. We haven't sorted the things stored there but there is no leakage or structural damage," Mr Semwal added sensing Arun's curiosity.

Arun nodded as they went into the bedroom upstairs. The bed was strung with rotting *niwar*, the coarse cotton tapes, which obviously needed replacement. Further beyond, there was a bathroom.

"I have had the plumbing checked. The pipes are okay. There were a few leakages here and there, but I have got them fixed," said Mr Semwal.

Arun was quite pleased by what he had seen. It appeared that the task of making Marilyn Villa habitable was less onerous than it appeared to be initially. He had a detailed discussion with Mr Semwal about what had to be done before his next visit to Mussoorie the coming year. He also spoke to the chowkidar who cheered up considerably when he learnt what his new salary would be, and that Mr Semwal would repair the outhouse as well. He fell at Arun's feet—his eyes wet with tears thinking about his good fortune.

Arun and his wife Maya travelled to Mussoorie in April. Winter had receded, but there was still a crisp, cool breeze with blue skies and magnificent views to enjoy. They came to Dehradun by train and hired two taxis to Mussoorie. A nurse accompanied them, along with a manservant who was primarily a cook but also doubled as a general factotum. They walked up to Marilyn Villa from Palladium Cinema past the church and up the steep hill past Wild Rose Villa. Arun and the servants walked, but he had arranged for a palanquin for Maya. Four coolies were needed to carry their luggage up the steep path to their new home.

Maya had been quiet and morose throughout the long journey. She could sense that they were leaving home, and the thought was unsettling. Arun and the nurse spoke soothingly to her and held her hand through the two long nights and days that the train journey had taken from

Bombay. She lay quietly in the palanquin and looked at the majestic deodar trees on the way to their new home. The beautiful hillsides with the rows of wild roses just beginning to bloom were equally captivating. She was able to walk a little, but the climb was too much for her fragile body, so Arun had decided to take a palanquin for her.

Maya got out of the palanquin when they reached the house and walked in with the nurse behind her. She went outside to the top of the stone staircase and sat down on the first step. The nurse hurried to cover her frail shoulders with a shawl. Maya was now sitting in her new home for the first time with the frou frou of the wind blowing through the deodar trees in her ears and the scent of the new wild rose blossoms in her nostrils.

Maya appeared to be comfortable in her new surroundings. The weather seemed to suit her, and she started eating and sleeping better. The days passed quickly with Arun trying to get the house in good shape. She spent most of the day near the staircase looking out over the mountains. At night, she slept in the downstairs bedroom. The nurse slept on a folding bed in the same room, while Arun slept upstairs. One morning when the nurse woke up, she found Maya sitting up in bed. She had a slight smile on her face and was cuddling a ragged doll.

"Where did you get the doll from?"

Maya did not answer. She clutched the doll even more closely as if she was afraid that it would be taken away from her. The nurse smiled and patted her hand

and said soothingly, "Don't worry, I won't take the doll away from you."

The nurse did not mention the matter to Arun as she thought that maybe Maya had got the doll from one of the servant's children from a neighbouring house. Maya seemed to be happy with the doll and that was what mattered. She would spend the day cuddling the doll while sitting at the top of the staircase. She smiled a little these days and even Dr Prasad who came to see her from St Catherine's Hospital seemed happy to see her improvement.

"I think the change of climate and the atmosphere here has done her good," said Dr Prasad.

Arun shook hands with the doctor and saw him to the door. He was smiling too.

That night, the nurse thought she heard a sound, so she got up only to find that Maya was sleeping peacefully. The nurse went back to sleep without thinking about it any further. Next morning, by the time she woke up, Maya had already got out of bed. Suddenly worried, the nurse hurriedly put on a wrap and went out of the bedroom to look for her. She found her sitting in her usual place at the top of the staircase. As she went closer, she saw that Maya had now found a little wooden bed for her doll. She had placed the doll on the tiny bed, and was singing to it a lullaby as old as time, all the while gently stroking the doll's hair.

Lalla lalla lori
Doodh ki katori
Doodh mein batasha

Munni kare tamasha

The nurse paused at the front door. She looked at Maya but did not disturb her. Arun tiptoed to the nurse and gestured her to follow him inside.

"Where did she get the doll and the bed from?" he asked.

"I don't know, sir. She got the doll a few days ago. I thought that one of the servants' children from the neighbouring houses might have given it to her—but now she has the bed too ..." said the nurse worriedly.

"You should have told me about it at once," said Arun a bit abruptly. "Please ask the servants, especially the old chowkidar whether they know anything about it."

After a couple of hours, the nurse came back after talking to all the servants. "Nobody knows anything about it," she said.

"That's strange. Where could Maya have found these things?" Arun asked in a puzzled voice.

"I think the old chowkidar knows something—something that he is not telling us," the nurse added after a moment of hesitation.

"But what makes you think so? Anyway, he is a strange fellow and I doubt if he will talk if he does not want to."

"I will search the house, and I will keep a closer watch on madam, sir," said the nurse.

There were no untoward incidents for the next few days. Maya was much more cheerful. She talked a little to Arun and the nurse, but kept to herself most of the time, crooning and talking to the doll. Soon it was May and the weather turned warmer. The sunshine was balmy, and every afternoon Arun would sit under the shade of a deodar tree, reading a book and watching his wife play with her doll.

"What's her name?" Arun gently asked one afternoon.

"Her name is Marilyn," said Maya in a perfectly clear voice.

Arun was amazed. Maya had not spoken so clearly in a long time. "Like the house?" Arun's question went unanswered, for Maya did not seem to be paying any heed to it.

That afternoon, clouds started gathering in the valley. By evening, thunder and lightning gave way to the first drops of a pre-monsoon shower. Soon it was raining heavily and, as is the practice in the hills, the electric power was switched off by the municipality. A few candles and a kerosene lamp provided some light as everyone prepared to go to bed early. Soon, with the soothing pitter-patter of the rain on the tin roof, they were all fast asleep.

It was the sound of the bedroom door banging in the breeze that woke up the nurse. She could barely see anything, so she lit a candle, only to see that Maya was not in bed. She had been half expecting this, so it took her very little time to come outside to find the front door open. It was still raining as she shouted for Arun and the chowkidar to come to her aid. Arun came down the stairs very quickly, almost as if he had been awake the entire time. He gauged the situation immediately and picked up a torch from the table in the hallway. He also put on a raincoat and gum boots before venturing out. The nurse followed his lead and the two came out of the house, to the top of the staircase.

It was raining heavily, and they could barely see. Shouting Maya's name, they hurried down the staircase to the road below. As they reached the road, the chowkidar met them. He was carrying a lantern and an umbrella. He had walked down the road from the outhouse and had reached there quickly after sensing the commotion inside the house. He gestured for the other two to follow him as he treaded down the path from the road. It was dark and slippery, but he obviously knew the way. Soon he stopped and pointed ahead. They could discern a figure dressed in a white nightgown just below them.

Maya stood motionless. She was looking down at the valley below, and for a moment Arun thought she might jump down into the abyss. He started taking slow steps towards her. As soon as he came close enough, he held her arm and pulled her close to him. He could feel her body shivering. Very gently, he drew her away from the precipice and started walking back with her, the chowkidar leading the way with his lantern. The nurse had hurried on ahead and was holding a large towel as Maya and Arun entered the drawing room. She wrapped it around Maya and took her into her bedroom.

When they came out, Maya was dry and had changed into another nightdress, wearing a warm wrap. The nurse led her to a chair near the fireplace where the chowkidar had lit a fire. By now, the whole household was awake, and the cook had made tea for everyone. Arun poured a cup of tea for Maya. She took the cup and said, "Thank you."

Those simple words almost brought tears to Arun's eyes. It had been years since Maya had acknowledged his presence.

Maya spoke again, "That poor child."

"Whom are you referring to?" Arun asked, though he already suspected the answer.

"Marilyn."

She stopped talking for a while until Arun asked her, "What happened to her?"

"She died," said Maya. Her voice broke as she continued, "She was so little." The effort it took to talk was taking a toll on her. She looked tired and spent.

Arun looked at the nurse and said, "I think you should take her to bed and let her rest."

He then turned towards the chowkidar after the two women had left the room. "You obviously know what happened. Tell me the whole story."

"Saheb, I am sorry that I did not tell you this before. Many people who came to buy the house went away after they heard the story. I did not want you too to leave."

"That does not matter now. Tell me the whole truth," said Arun in a firm voice.

"The gora saheb, Mackintosh saheb, lived here before Independence. The house was not called Marilyn Villa in those days. They were a childless couple and were overjoyed when their daughter was born after many years. They named her Marilyn," said the chowkidar, sitting on his haunches a little away from the carpet. He took a sip of his tea and continued, "Mackintosh saheb called a priest from the church after the child's christening. He wanted him to bless the house as he had renamed it Marilyn Villa."

There was a brief silence in the room. The rain had died down and the flickering flames of the fire crackled gently. Arun got up and poured a tot of rum for the chowkidar and himself. He handed the glass to the chowkidar and said, "What happened after that?"

"Marilyn was a delightful, beautiful child. My wife was her maid, and she was totally devoted to her. Little Marilyn was very independent and was fond of running around. My wife was constantly running behind her. One day, when she was around three, she ran off to the road with my wife at her heels. Before she could catch up with her, Marilyn slipped and fell off the mountain. She died that day, saheb," said the chowkidar in a trembling voice. "The whole household was plunged into gloom after this awful event. Mackintosh saheb began drinking heavily and Maya memsaheb withdrew completely into herself."

"What did you say?" Arun asked sharply.

"Yes, saheb, the gora memsaheb's name was also Maya."

Arun was quite shaken by the turn of events. He got up and refilled both their glasses and remained standing, facing the fire.

"Maya memsaheb's condition became steadily worse. Many doctors and priests came to see her but there was no improvement. One day, on a night like this when it was raining heavily, she walked out of the house and jumped off the cliff at the same place where her daughter had fallen," said the chowkidar. The gora saheb shut down the house and left soon afterwards. Marilyn missy's toys and clothes were carefully packed by my wife and stored in the cellar below. Nobody had found them until now," the chowkidar's voice trailed off.

There was nothing more to say. The rain had stopped, and the clouds had cleared up. Streaks of dawn were already lightening the eastern horizon. The chowkidar got up, took his leave with a *salaam*, and left for the outhouse to get some sleep if he could. Arun sat down and continued to stare at the dying fire as it spluttered and crackled. He must have fallen asleep, for when he opened his eyes, his wife was standing beside him with her arm on his shoulder. The nurse was standing a little behind. Maya was dressed in khaki trousers and a pullover, and her hair was neatly combed.

She smiled at him and said, "I did not want to wake you up, but it's such a beautiful day and I thought we could go for a walk."

Arun got up stiffly, rubbing his shoulder. He said with a wide smile, "Give me a moment to freshen up and I will be right back."

3

Dilkusha Estate

Nawab Sirajuddin was a careful man. His detractors would insist that he was miserly and petty-minded, but he prided himself on the husbanding of his not inconsiderable fortune in the troubled days when politicians exhorted you to miss a meal for the sake of the country. Nawab Sirajuddin may have had a vague idea about the goings-on in the country, but he was absolutely clear about his own interests, which focused on saving every penny he had, including those that he did not have now but may have had in the past or was likely to acquire in future. He economised on everything—his household, his servants, and himself. It was rumoured that he had worn the same pyjamas and *achkan* for the last twenty years, but this could not be verified. Certainly, his black achkan had worn out, shiny patches on it and his pyjamas had turned a delicate shade of yellow but that may have been just a coincidence.

His only recreation when he was not poring over his books on accounts was chess. He invariably played with his lifelong friend. Mirza Akhtar Rehman had never married and was almost a permanent resident at the nawab's haveli in Lucknow. He was a very different kettle of fish than the miserly nawab. Fond of dancing girls, music, Urdu poetry, and wine, he was amiably running through his family fortune, much to the dismay of his parsimonious friend.

Nawab saheb had inherited Dilkusha Estate in Mussoorie from his grandfather. It was a rambling structure just below Camel's Back Road near the *chhattri*. His father had died, when he was still a boy, perhaps from an overdose of opium or scotch whisky, both of which he was much addicted to. The youthful Sirajuddin, seeing his father's pitiable demise, firmly turned his back on the pleasures of the flesh at a very young age.

Sirajuddin had always been a serious boy and after his father's death, he became positively puritanical. His only real friend was the mirza whom he cherished as his own brother. He had married late, a woman not from his own social status and with whom he did not really share a rapport beyond the humdrum necessities of running a household. The poor woman was condemned to a life of domestic drudgery, with even the saving grace of motherhood denied to her. If you were charitable, you could feel sorry for the nawab, but most people either despised or ignored him.

Over the years, the original rooms in Dilkusha Estate had been partitioned and subdivided, giving the impression of an unplanned rabbit warren. Sirajuddin's grandfather had four wives with numerous progeny (all female, much to his dismay, other than the solitary male black sheep, Sirajuddin's father, being the youngest), so the house had to be modified from its original design to accommodate all the squabbling brood. It was incongruously built like a

Lucknow haveli and looked out of place in the Himalayan landscape. It did not even have the obligatory sloping, red-painted tin roof but a flat terrace instead that groaned under the weight of the snow in winters. The occupants shivered in the open passages and the courtyard, all of which were better designed for a balmy evening in Awadh. There was a large outhouse also, where the nawab's hangers-on, servants, and a few ageing *tawaifs* who had caught the old man's fancy resided in accustomed squalor.

It was a chaotic household, and when Sirajuddin had finally taken charge after his grandfather's death, he had almost torn his hair out in frustration. Starting with his grandmothers and their families, he gradually succeeded in getting them to vacate. After all, it is a bit difficult to stay in a house without electricity and water, especially in the midst of a Himalayan winter. The evicted family members cursed him, but he was indifferent to their lamentations and his tactics ultimately bore fruit.

Finally, as the 1960s dawned, he was the only inhabitant left in Dilkusha Estate. He adopted a different approach to the outhouse. He imposed a rent on all the inhabitants and enforced it diligently, using the might of *pahalwans* he had brought in from Lucknow. That drove off most of the hangers-on and left only a few who could afford to pay—contretemps that delighted the stingy nawab.

Mirza Saheb looked on with amusement at his friend's shenanigans. He often asked the nawab what and whom he was doing all this for. He was childless, after all, and preserving and growing his already vast fortune seemed a bit pointless. These discussions invariably took place after the mandatory chess game, played either in the nawab's haveli in Lucknow or at Dilkusha Estate, where the mirza was the only friend who was invited to share the nawab's seclusion.

The nawab was always a bit more receptive if he won, so the canny mirza made sure he lost when he had to convey something of import. Of late, these discussions had become even more infructuous than usual, so the mirza chose to retire behind an amiable alcoholic haze rather than continue to needle his recalcitrant friend.

One evening in May, after the game of chess had been concluded at Dilkusha Estate and the two friends were reclining at ease before dinner, their peace was rudely shattered.

A young woman rushed in, screaming, "They are beating her! They're taking her away!"

Startled, the two men turned to her. With her bosom heaving, tears running down her cheeks, dishevelled hair, the unveiled young woman was quite a fulsome apparition. They got up and stood staring as she continued to scream and beat her head.

"What's the matter? Who is being beaten?" the mirza asked. He had an appreciative gleam in his eye at the feminine pulchritude on display.

"My mother, please save her!" the woman cried. She came forward and fell at the nawab's feet, knowing him to be the master. He flinched and recoiled but held his ground. Bending down, he tried to lift the young woman, but she refused to let go of his feet, sobbing all the while. With some difficulty, he managed to disengage himself and the two men walked out of the house behind the distraught young woman. She ran out of the back door straight to the outhouse.

There were quite a few people watching as the pahalwans were throwing out the pathetic debris of a penurious human existence from one of the little rooms of the outhouse. One of the pahalwans was holding an elderly woman in a vice-like grip while the others did their work of emptying out her quarters. The young woman ran to the pahalwan holding her mother and began beating him with her puny fists.

The pahalwan was a huge man with a large moustache. He laughed loudly at this unexpected assault and fended the young woman off with a swipe from his left hand. She was flung away and, in falling, hit her head against a stone balustrade. She lay there, insensible, with a little trickle of blood on her forehead. All this happened literally within seconds. Rather surprisingly, the mirza found himself outpaced by his normally languid friend.

"What's happening here?" the nawab addressed his question to one of the pahalwans.

"Huzoor, this woman has not been paying her rent, so we are throwing out both her and her daughter as per your orders," said the pahalwan obsequiously.

"It's been only a month late, huzoor," protested the elderly woman. "I did not get enough work for my sewing, so I asked for a postponement. But these animals have thrown all my belongings out. What will happen to me and Razia?" With that, the elderly woman started weeping loudly and beating her chest, having been released by the pahalwan.

The nawab turned his attention to the young woman who was sprawled on the ground. He went to her and held her head while calling for water to be brought. One of the bystanders quickly fetched water in a brass lota. The nawab sprinkled some droplets over the young woman's face and soon her eyelids flickered. She opened her eyes with a soft moan to see the nawab looking down at her solicitously.

The mirza was watching this tender scene with growing amusement. He motioned to the pahalwans to back off; and seeing which way the tide was turning, they were happy to be on their way. The elderly woman came forward and fell at the nawab's feet.

"Save us, huzoor, you are our *annadaata*, our benefactor," said the elderly woman in a trembling voice. "I have faithfully served you for many years."

"You are Aasma-apa, aren't you?" the nawab said in an astonished voice.

"It is very kind of you to remember my name and to address me as a sister," said the elderly woman. Though she was dressed in rags, there was nonetheless a certain dignity about her. She spoke with an educated accent. Intrigued, the mirza came closer to listen to the conversation.

"I did not know you were living here," said the nawab. "I thought you were in Lucknow."

"It is not in our fate to be noticed by fortunate people like you," said Aasma. If there was a twinge of sarcasm in her voice, who would grudge her that infinitesimal pleasure. "I came back here many years ago, Nawab saheb. It is not easy being poor in Lucknow where everyone knows you and points fingers at you either out of contempt or misplaced pity. I had lived in this house before, but it is a different experience living in the outhouse." She turned towards her daughter and with gentle strength drew her towards herself.

"We will leave the outhouse if you so wish, Nawab saheb," said Aasma.

The nawab stood there without speaking. Finally, the mirza intervened, "There is no need to leave immediately. Please go back to your quarters. I will speak to Nawab saheb, and he will let you know his decision tomorrow morning." With that, the mirza drew his friend back to the house.

They sat down by the chess table. The mirza poured himself some whisky and, after looking at his friend's tired visage, offered him some as well. Rather surprisingly, he accepted and the two friends sat in silence for a while, mulling over the events of the last hour.

"Who is Aasma and why did you call her apa?" the mirza asked. It was the question uppermost in his mind.

"Do you remember Salma-apa?" the nawab questioned.

"Of course. She was your sister. Didn't she get married to that man from Hyderabad? Suleiman?"

"Yes, as you know, he turned out to be a scoundrel. When he died, my sister came back to Lucknow as she could not bear to live with his family in Hyderabad any more. My grandfather was very upset, but he supported her decision," said the nawab.

"What does that have to do with Aasma?"

"Suleiman married Aasma against his family's wishes after his marriage to my sister, as my sister could not beget any children. Suleiman and Aasma had a child, Razia, whom you just saw. For some reason, my sister really liked Aasma, and when she came back to Lucknow, she brought her and the child along," said the nawab.

"Remarkable! For a woman to bring her *sautan* home, along with her stepchild, is quite unheard of. I know that Salma-apa was an amazing lady, but this is phenomenal," said Mirza saheb admiringly.

"What happened after that?"

The nawab paused for a while. There were some things that he had not shared with even his best friend. Finally, he spoke, "My grandfather died, and I was the only male heir, so I inherited everything. I had a very difficult time sorting out his estate and getting rid of the hangers-on." He stopped speaking and looked away.

"You don't need to worry about what you did so long ago. You can tell me," said the mirza gently.

"I threw my sister out of the house," said the nawab at last in a trembling voice. "She died soon afterwards. Aasma-apa and her daughter went with my sister. I did not bother to find out where they went. I was obsessed with my inheritance and growing wealth."

There was a complete silence after he finished speaking. The mirza was lost for words and the nawab's eyes were wet with tears of remorse.

The two friends met late the next day. Mirza saheb had slept heavily and made an appearance only at noon. He found his friend sitting in the drawing room and reading an Urdu newspaper.

The nawab looked at him as he walked in and said, "I have made a decision about Aasma-apa and Razia." There was an unaccustomed smile on his face and his whole demeanour seemed to have undergone a change for the better.

"Well?"

"I have asked them to move out of the outhouse," said the nawab.

"I see," said the mirza non-committally.

"I have asked them to move into the main house," said the nawab with a laugh. "See, here they are!"

The two men got up as the women entered the room. No longer dressed in rags, the mother–daughter duo looked ethereal. As they came closer, the nawab ushered them to a sofa, where they sat for a while without speaking. A servant brought in tea in a silver teapot and Aasma-apa poured it out for all of them.

"Your house is beautiful, Nawab saheb. It is so much better than when I lived here many years ago," said Aasma as she passed them their cups. Razia got up and walked to the window from where a magnificent view of the snow-capped hills was visible. The nawab followed her with his eyes, put down his cup and eventually joined her at the window.

Mirza saheb watched his friend with a quizzical smile on his face and turned towards Aasma-apa. She was smiling too.

4

Eunice Pond

Nobody knew why the house was called Eunice Pond. There was certainly no pond there and if there had ever been a Eunice, she wasn't around any more. The house stood below the level of the main road as it wound its leisurely way from Library to the Wild Rose Hotel. It had remained unoccupied for several years. The overgrown garden, flaking plaster and rusting tin roof looked forlorn and neglected, though it had been an elegant house in earlier years. There was a semicircular veranda with a red oxide floor and a sloping tin roof supported by pillars overlooking the garden and the mountains beyond. French windows opened on to the veranda from the drawing room. The house was two-storeyed and had stables and an outhouse for servants at the back.

The new owners had had the walls painted with a brighter shade of yellow than intended. Even the fresh colour of the red tin roof was somehow different from the roofs of the other houses around. The new owners were cheerful folk. The man dressed in a bright checked coat with a tweed cap looked like a caricature of an army colonel, with his bushy moustache and loud voice. His polished brown shoes seemed just a shade the wrong colour to go with his tight grey flannel trousers. He was a short, stout person with a strutting, ungainly walk. His beady eyes and piercing gaze belied the benign image that he tried to project.

His wife had hennaed hair coifed into an unlikely bun. She also wore trousers, their size indicative more of hope than reality. They gave her a strange waddling gait, accentuated by the unsuitable high heels that she wore all the time. Her overlarge diamond earrings and the glittering solitaire on her gnarled ring finger clearly proclaimed that she was not just the wife of a penurious retired army colonel. She had a raucous voice with a tendency to mispronounce a few words. Twenty would become "twentai" and Dehradun lost its musical softness by becoming "Deradoon" with a hard D.

The Mehrotras, the new owners of Eunice Pond, had first arrived early one summer in a two-toned green Studebaker station wagon with white sidewall tyres, driven by a chauffeur wearing a khaki uniform and a peaked cap. The capacious boot of the car carried mountains of luggage, including a very large, old and heavy mahogany chest that was unloaded under the careful supervision of the chauffeur.

Their new house had been undergoing a major renovation in anticipation of their arrival. Carpenters, masons, decorators, plumbers, and workmen of all descriptions had been swarming all over the house since March. They were supervised by a thin, acerbic *munshi* who was always the first to arrive at the building site and the last to leave. He terrorised the workmen, many of whom were twice his size. Thanks to him, the work was mostly complete in time for the arrival of his masters. The Mehrotras returned to Delhi the same day after taking stock of the progress of the renovation work, as there was still a lot of unfinished business that they had to attend to before making the final shift. It was in mid-summer when they finally settled down in their new house.

There was a flurry of activity after the new owners arrived at Eunice Pond. The lady soon realised that it was important to have her own rickshaw for the evening promenade on the Mall Road. She could hardly walk along with the hoi polloi, could she? Accordingly, a new rickshaw was procured. It was painted a bright bottle green, again just a trifle different from the other rickshaws owned by the maharanis who frequented Mussoorie during the summertime. It had a crest of dubious origins painted on the side featuring a lion and a unicorn—obviously borrowed from English royalty—painted on one side.

If the maharanis found the new upstart amusing, they hid it well behind their dark glasses. The English having quit these shores many years ago, there was no one left to protest the impertinence. Her spouse found the evening promenade not to his liking. Most of the maharajas and other notables were on horseback, a skill that he was not conversant with. It was not considered de rigueur for men to sit in the rickshaw beside their wives, so he trailed disconsolately behind on foot for a few days but eventually gave up as he was hard put to keep up the pace.

He thus spent his evenings interfering with the household servants while his wife was away. In all likelihood, he enjoyed the proceedings, but his servants certainly did not. The Mehrotras' social endeavours met with mixed success. They were often seen at the Lexton Plaza and the White Palisades Hotel or the Mountain Range Club where all it took to gain entry was an adequate supply of coins of the realm. They made 'friends' who were quite happy to accept their hospitality at Eunice Pond but the more exclusive soirées of Mussoorie society were closed to them.

By October, most of the summer visitors had left. There had been a brief 'second season' at Dussehra, but this too soon died down. The Mehrotras displayed no inclination to leave. When questioned by some of their 'friends', they laughed and replied that they had come to Mussoorie for good and intended to stay there permanently. Even when their decision was considered unusual, nobody actually said so to their face. The couple dismissed most of their servants, only retaining the faithful munshi and the chauffeur.

It was a severe winter that year and while the Mehrotras made attempts to walk outside, these died down as the snow increased. The house wore a cloistered look until spring began to make its appearance in March. The snow melted, green shoots sprang up and gradually their old servants returned. The house began to look cheerful again.

It was in April when a visitor made her way to Eunice Pond late one morning. She was a young woman dressed in a printed silk sari with a coat and scarf to keep the cold wind at bay. She carried a small leather briefcase and was admitted into the house after a brief colloquy with the chauffeur, who opened the front gate after she had banged and shouted for quite a while. She was shown into the drawing room where she sat on a sofa facing the window. After a brief wait, the Mehrotras walked in to greet their unexpected guest. She had discarded her scarf and as she rose to meet them, they could see that she was an attractive lady, around thirty-five years old. She had shoulder-length hair, which she had left open, and wore a big red bindi on her forehead. She looked professional and competent.

"I am sorry to barge in like this," she said apologetically. "My name is Anita Pathak, and I am a journalist working with the *National Mail* in Delhi."

As she spoke, a frown gathered on the faces of the Mehrotras. Finally, Mr Mehrotra spoke in a measured way, "You have come here without an invitation, madam. We do not wish to talk to any reporters. It would be better if you leave immediately." His voice and tone seemed to have undergone a change. It no longer sounded boisterous or hectoring—instead, he sounded calm and in control.

"Here me out, sir," said Anita, undaunted.

"There is nothing to say," said Mrs Mehrotra. Even her voice had changed subtly. She stood up, her posture straight, with a purposeful gleam in her eye.

"Is it correct to say that your name is not Mehrotra?" Anita persisted.

"What we call ourselves is our choice, madam," replied Mr Mehrotra.

"Are you not from Delhi? You have a house in Jor Bagh, and your name is Srivastava?" Anita asked in an even tone.

All three were standing facing each other and the tension was palpable.

"What if it is?" Mr Mehrotra said challengingly. "I have already told you that what we call ourselves is our business."

"Is it not true that your teenaged daughter was murdered four years ago?" Anita went on.

"Yes, yes, yes! She was murdered! My innocent child was killed so brutally!" Mrs Mehrotra screamed suddenly. Her husband made a calming gesture and put his arm around his wife's shoulders.

"I am indeed sorry for your loss, madam. Perhaps you have not recognised me. I am one of the reporters who have been tracking this incident right from the beginning. I met you at your Jor Bagh residence too," said Anita.

"She was abducted when she was returning from her college—in broad daylight!" Mrs Srivastava was sobbing now. Her haunted eyes and broken voice spoke of the terrible pain that she had endured.

Aparna Srivastava was eighteen years old in 1959. She was the only child of her parents. Her father was a successful building contractor, and they lived in a beautiful new bungalow in Jor Bagh very near to Lodhi Gardens. After completing her schooling, Aparna had joined Lady Margaret College to study English literature. She used to go to college by bus as she felt that arriving in her parents' chauffeur-driven car was too ostentatious.

On 3 April, Aparna boarded a bus in front of her college in the afternoon. It broke down in a lonely area near the crematorium and all the passengers had to get down. One by one, they all left from there, either walking or some in autorickshaws. Aparna did not want to get into an autorickshaw on her own, but when there were very few people left, she finally got into one and it drove off towards Lodhi Road. That was the last time she was seen alive.

Her mutilated, naked body was discovered in the jungles near Mehrauli almost a week later. She had been repeatedly raped and then strangled. The police investigation finally led to the son of a politician who owned many autorickshaws and had a farmhouse near Mehrauli. The son was a debauch who used some of the autorickshaw drivers to procure women. Aparna had unfortunately boarded one of these autos. The driver had overpowered and drugged her and driven her to the farmhouse where the politician's son and his cronies had raped her for a few days. When they tired of her, the politician's son had strangled her and dumped her body in the jungles near the farmhouse.

The police managed to trace the auto driver based on the account of a witness who had seen Aparna boarding the auto and had remembered the number. The trail led to the farmhouse and eventually to Aparna's body. The politician's son had been arrested along with a few of his cronies. All this had happened in a very short time—barely a few weeks after Aparna had been abducted. The press was full of praise for the police and Aparna's unfortunate parents felt that justice, at least, had been meted out to their daughter's killer.

The trial dragged on for a long time. The politician provided incontrovertible evidence to prove that his son was not in Delhi on the day that Aparna was abducted. He was in Jaipur with his maternal uncle and had remained there the whole week. Many witnesses came forward to corroborate the story. The prosecution's case collapsed, and the prisoners were set free. Aparna's parents ran from pillar to post to get the case reopened but in the absence of fresh evidence, the courts declined their plea. Mr Srivastava found it difficult to get new contracts as the politician was a very powerful figure in Delhi circles and gradually, his business declined.

"Do you know that Ajay Chauhan disappeared about a year ago?" Anita asked. Ajay was the name of the politician's son.

Both husband and wife nodded.

"Yes, we did hear of it and in fact, the police came and met us. I suppose they thought we would be the prime suspects," said Mr Mehrotra, with a tinge of cynicism. "They knew that we had decided to move to Mussoorie. There were too many painful memories there, and we did not keep track of what happened to that scoundrel," said Mr Srivastava. "Was he eventually found?"

"No, he just disappeared. Finally, the police gave up as the trail ran cold," said Anita.

"Well, too bad for him,"Mr Srivastava added with a shrug.

"Why have you changed your names?" Anita couldn't stop herself from wondering aloud.

"We did not want anybody to find us," said Mrs Srivastava. "How did you find us, by the way?"

"It was not difficult. I did learn that you had sold your house. You had told the broker to find a house for you in Mussoorie. Through him I contacted the broker in Mussoorie whom you had approached for buying this house and he confirmed that you had purchased the house under your real names," said Anita.

"We had told the broker not to tell anyone!" Mrs Srivastava exclaimed.

"It's not easy to resist questioning by a trained reporter," said Anita with a laugh.

By now, the constraints between them had lifted somewhat. Tea had been brought in, and the conversation had become more relaxed.

"Can we rely on you not to tell the world about where we are? We really do want to leave the past behind," said Mrs Srivastava pleadingly.

Anita rose to leave. She nodded and held out her hand. Both husband and wife shook hands with her and started walking with her to show her out.

As she went towards the door being held open by Mr Srivastava, her gaze fell on the large mahogany chest that had been placed under an open window. On it was an exquisite statue of Durga, the slayer of demons.

5

Bushmills Lodge

The original owner of Bushmills Lodge obviously missed the smooth Irish whisky of his homeland. One can only hope that he had imported many cases of the ambrosial spirit and that the mists and green hills of Mussoorie were a good substitute for the Northern Irish countryside. Be that as it may, he was now long gone, and the origins of the house's name were only known to the cognoscenti.

The lodge was set above the main road as it wound its way from the Wild Rose Hotel to the Company Bagh. It was beautifully maintained, with white-painted railings and a circular veranda on the first floor. The roof was painted green—in contrast to the red roofs that generally prevailed—perhaps by the original owner in another nostalgic memory of his Celtic home; and successive owners had followed the same practice. The gravel driveway leading up to the house ended in a little circle with a small marble fountain in the middle. There was a large garden graced by a magnolia tree on one side with rose bushes at the other end.

An incongruous setting indeed for the dumpy, weather-beaten form of Chinmayi as she sat on a wooden bench at the far end of the garden. As always, she was untidily dressed in denim overalls and a Fair Isle sweater. She was wearing gardening boots, and a basket full of gardening tools lay unattended on the lawn nearby. Her wispy hair had a few strands of grey, carelessly concealed behind an old straw hat framing her round face. The flower beds needed attention, but Chinmayi sat there, unheeding. She had kindly eyes, but today they looked ahead without seeing. She was not attractive, far from it, but there was something appealing about her personality.

"Nalini mata-ji has come to see you, Bibi-ji," said Damyanti in Hindi as she came close to where Chinmayi was sitting.

With a sigh, Chinmayi nodded and got up slowly. She was not sure how people had come to know about her knowledge of homeopathy. She had told nobody, for sure, but a trickle of people had started coming to see her soon after she had arrived in Mussoorie. She was not a qualified homeopath, and she had been careful about specifying that to everyone, but they did not seem to care. The trickle was in danger of becoming an influx.

Chinmayi walked across the garden into the veranda. To the right was a little sitting room that had become a sort of a consultation room almost by default. It was a cosy, feminine room. As she entered, Nalini got up slowly to greet her.

Chinmayi went forward and took the old lady's hand. "Please do sit down," she said in a soft voicc.

Nalini looked at her fondly and patted her hand. "Beti, the medicine you gave me has worked very well. My arthritis is so much better that I can actually walk!" The joy and excitement in the older lady's voice was palpable. "I came to thank you." She beamed at Chinmayi and, drawing her closer, kissed her on her forehead.

"I will give you some follow-up medicine, mata-ji. Here, please take this twice a day before lunch and dinner," said Chinmayi.

"And what should I pay you?" Nalini asked.

"Nothing, nothing. I am not a qualified homeopathic doctor anyway. This is just my hobby," said Chinmayi, with a self-depreciating gesture.

"Who needs qualified doctors! I have been going to Dr Banerjee in Kulri for years, but his medicine just does not work!" Nalini exclaimed as she got up to go.

Chinmayi took her hand and guided her to the rickshaw that was waiting for her. She waved as the old lady left and then slowly turned around and walked inside the house.

Ajit had left for work after breakfast. He was a master at Regency Park School and the walk to work took him around the winding road to Library and then down the Mall Road. He had been a professor at Delhi University till last year. He was a historian with a postgraduate degree from Cambridge University. Overqualified to be a master at Regency Park? Perhaps, but life has a way of dealing a set of cards that you cannot always predict.

He walked briskly, trying to still his turbulent thoughts. He had broken the news to Chinmayi at the breakfast table, though he had received Avantika's letter the previous day. He had prevaricated, not telling her the entire truth, but the essential fact that Chinmayi had to leave Bushmills Lodge could not be avoided. The wind whistled around him and his muffler flapped in the breeze as he walked through the narrow lane opening on to Library. It was not crowded, being early in the season, and he walked fast, without the press of people and rickshaws hindering his progress. He went past the shops after Library, Palladium Cinema and Doon View Skating rink, with barely a pause before descending to the school.

The neatly ordered buildings, gravel paths and seasonal flowers in their well-kept beds were a balm to his chaotic thoughts. The school was his refuge. In his little study, he could let his mind wander and dwell on the more pleasant aspects of his life. He could handle the school-level classes without effort, what worried him was his book on ancient India—he had hardly been able to make any progress on it since he had shifted to Mussoorie last year. He had decided to buy Bushmills Lodge and had resigned from Delhi University, planning to spend most of his time in the hills. If he had hoped that the cool mountain air would clear the cobwebs from his mind and promote creative thought, he may have been asking for too much.

Chinmayi climbed up the wooden staircase reluctantly. She walked into the bedroom where an open suitcase lay waiting for her to finish her packing. Without conscious thought, she mechanically folded her few clothes and stuffed them into the suitcase. Not given to the use of feminine cosmetics and blandishments, the bathroom counter was also soon cleared of her belongings. Feeling breathless, she sat down on the edge of the bed and looked outside the window, on to the sunlit garden where she had been sitting earlier.

"Why are you packing, Bibi-ji?" Damyanti said as she came into the room. "Are you leaving us?" She spoke in a solicitous tone and there was genuine affection in her voice. In fact, the reason why Chinmayi's reputation as a homeopath had spread was that she had helped Damyanti's son in quickly recovering from an attack of whooping cough. Damyanti had been effusive in her praise for Chinmayi, and her fame had soon spread across the hill station.

"Yes, I am leaving."

"But why?"

"I have to go,"

"But you never told me that you were going. Has something happened?" Damyanti asked insistently.

A small frown gathered on Chinmayi's forehead, and she spoke with mild reproof, "I've already told you that I have to go. Nothing has happened." Her uncharacteristically brusque tone was enough for Damyanti to stop asking further questions.

Chinmayi finished her packing sooner than expected. Damyanti was waiting for her at the foot of the stairs and as Chinmayi nodded, she went upstairs to fetch her suitcase. The driver had already brought out the black

Envoy car and very soon, Chinmayi walked outside and got into the back seat. She waved goodbye to the maid as the driver drove the car out of the front gate and down to the main road. As the car turned the corner and she could no longer see Bushmills Lodge, she found that her eyes were wet with tears. Soon the car was on the way to Dehradun, well in time for Chinmayi to catch the night train to Delhi.

Ajit returned home late that evening. It was already dark by the time he walked into the house. A single light was burning in the dining room, and the table was laid for only one person. He gazed at the table with a vacant expression as Damyanti walked in and switched on some lights, dispelling the gloom.

"Bibi-ji has left, saheb," she announced in a voice where accusation, sadness and trepidation were somehow mingled.

"Yes, I know," said Ajit tiredly. He was in no mood for a conversation with Damyanti, especially when he could sense the reproach in her tone. After having his dinner, he went upstairs to face the loneliness of the night.

The next day passed and so did the one after that. It almost seemed that Bushmills Lodge was falling into a routine again when on Saturday, a car drove up the drive. It was a sky-blue Chevrolet Impala, complete with tail fins, a long bonnet and a boot to match. It was driven by a chauffeur wearing a white uniform and a peaked cap. He quickly got out of his seat as the car crunched to a halt on the gravel and opened the back door for his passenger to alight.

The woman was wearing a rose-pink chiffon sari with a printed blouse. Her carefully coiffured hair fell in graduated waves down to her shoulders and a magnificent travelling cape from the fur of some unfortunate animal was draped around her elegant shoulders. Her rosebud mouth was curled into a discontented pout as she alighted with her hand on the chauffeur's arm to get support. She surveyed the building and gardens with a disdainful sweep of her eyes before pushing up her Christian Dior sunglasses up to her forehead, where they lay perched with the small diamonds set in the frame glinting in the sunlight.

Damyanti came running out of the house to greet the unexpected guest. "Namaste, memsaheb."

"Who are you?" the lady asked as she looked up and down at Damyanti.

"I am Damyanti, memsaheb. I look after the house and do the cooking," said Damyanti eagerly.

"Well, bring in the luggage."

"Avantika! I was not expecting you before Sunday!" Ajit said as he walked out of the house. He went up and put his arms around her while she offered her cheek for him to kiss.

"Well, here I am, darling." Avantika's voice was a slow drawl. "I'm starving. There was nothing to eat on the way."

"There are hundreds of dhabas on the roadside," said Ajit laughing.

"You surely don't expect me to eat at a dhaba," said Avantika. She laughed too, but there was an edge in her voice. "You seem to have settled in quite nicely here. It's just as well that I left you alone while you were setting it all up."

"The old owners had kept it in very good repair. I only needed to move in the furniture, and got some local servants to help for that," said Ajit.

"I wonder who will now provide us with a gourmet meal," remarked Avantika a shade sarcastically.

"That may be asking for too much, but Damyanti is a very good cook," said Ajit defensively.

"Well, let's see," said Avantika dismissively. "She seems like a total *dehati*."

She walked into the house with Ajit behind her. Damyanti was just ahead of them, struggling with a heavy suitcase that the chauffeur had handed over to her. She dragged the suitcase upstairs and the moment it hit the bannisters, it evoked a sharp rebuke from Avantika.

"How clumsy can you get! If anything breaks inside, you will be responsible."

"Shall we have lunch immediately?" Ajit asked.

"Didn't you hear when I said that I'm starving? Let that dumb woman first come downstairs," said Avantika cuttingly.

Damyanti came down meekly in a few moments. Even though she could not understand the conversation, as it was in English, the import of the tone and the words was clear enough. Her ears were burning as she hurried into the kitchen to bring out the food.

Lunch was a quick affair but did not end before Avantika had criticised the choice of dishes, the way the table was laid, the way the food was served, and obviously the way it tasted. Damyanti was almost in tears by the time lunch was over and Avantika went upstairs.

"Where the hell is my suitcase, you idiot!" Avantika screamed from above.

"It's in the guest room, memsaheb," stammered Damyanti as she ran up the stairs, with Ajit behind her.

"Why have you put it there? You are a complete fool," shouted Avantika. "Bring it here immediately."

'Here' was the master bedroom where she was standing with her hands on her hips in the middle of the room. Damyanti dragged the suitcase out of the guest room and into the master bedroom, and made good her escape to the servant's quarters. She was trembling and tearful when her husband found her lying curled up on their bed.

"What happened?"

"She is a terrible woman," Damyanti said between sobs. She started sobbing and her husband put his arms around her. "I can't believe that saheb would want another woman like her. She is so awful. His wife is such a wonderful person."

"Whom are you referring to?" her husband asked.

"Why, Chinmayi bibi-ji, of course! With such a wonderful wife, why would anyone take a mistress as terrible as this one," said Damyanti.

Her husband paused before he answered. He had spoken at length to the chauffeur who had explained the entire matter to him.

"Damyanti, Avantika memsaheb is his wife. It's Chinmayi bibi-ji who is his mistress," he said gently.

6

Pine Woods Estate

Pine Woods House was one of the first houses to come up on Camel's Back Road. Built on expansive lines using local stone, the turreted house had pretensions of looking like a castle. It was established in the first half of the nineteenth century just below the road. What was intriguing and just a little eerie was the location, right beside the Parsi graveyard with not even a wall in between. The extensive grounds of Pine Woods Estate went down into the valley, skirting the boundary of the graveyard all the way down the hill.

The house had been built by Henry Tavistock, a self-taught cartographer associated with George Everest. He had been an adventurer of sorts prior to his government job, but nobody seemed to know exactly what he did earlier. He certainly had more money than his government job was paying him. Perhaps the bleak and desolate countryside of Henry's home in Devon had moved him to find an isolated location for his house in Mussoorie. His work took him to Everest's house at Hathi Paon that was a long ride away, so instead of returning back the same day, he'd spend many nights billeted in his office.

Engaged in conducting the great trigonometric survey of India, George Everest was rarely present in Mussoorie, so Henry had the place to himself often enough. Henry had married early, but his wife balked at the long sea voyage around the Cape of Good Hope to India, and was content to remain in England with her son William.

Henry, beset by loneliness in India, had only two distractions: the *lal sharab*, the claret that many Englishmen were fond of drinking, and the Pahadi women whom he found to be maddeningly alluring. The latter addiction finally led him to Basanti, one of two beautiful sisters who were the daughters of a forest contractor whom Henry had approached for clearing the trees in place of which his house was to be constructed. The normal blandishments of white privilege, bluster and money signally failed to move the beauty and her unyielding father. They belonged to an influential, upper-caste family and liaisons of the type that Henry was used to were completely ruled out.

Finally, worn down by his solitude and dreams of connubial bliss, he proposed marriage. This was carried out in formal style when he visited the contractor's house beyond Mussoorie Library with a retinue and gifts for his bride-to-be and her family. He was received ceremoniously and his proposal was accepted after due consideration. The couple was married with Hindu rituals in the bride's house, as is customary, with Henry's servants serving as the *baraat*. His British friends looked askance at his doings and refused to attend the nuptials.

Eventually, as is often the case, the rumour mills tired of the scandal. Meanwhile, the second Mrs Tavistock was duly installed as the mistress of Pine Woods Estate. In the fullness of time, she presented her husband with two sons. They were named Robert and Anand.

The momentous events of 1857 largely passed by Mussoorie, and life continued apace. However, Henry was now approaching retirement age, and he found that the new administration under the British Crown looked askance at liaisons such as his. He also found himself missing the fog and environs of home. On the surface, Henry was a respectable man who had amassed a respectable fortune in India. Both his families, abroad as well as the one in India, appeared to be well looked after. Finally, he made up his mind to go back to England.

"It's only for a while," he told his wife Basanti placatingly in Hindustani. She had learnt English but spoke it haltingly. She had taken to wearing Western clothes and with her fine Pahadi features and erect posture, she looked regal and beautiful at the same time.

"I will take Robert with me, " he continued. "Now, with the opening of the Suez Canal, the whole journey will take just a month," said Henry. Basanti looked at him reproachfully but did not say anything.

Henry and Robert left for England in two weeks. Basanti never saw them again.

Time passed. A little more than a hundred years later, an Englishman and his wife checked in to Lexton Plaza Hotel in Mussoorie. He gave their names as Sir Henry and Lady Mary Tavistock.

Sir Henry met the Swiss manager of the hotel in his room soon after checking in.

"Is there a house in Mussoorie called Pine Woods Estate?" Henry asked after the obligatory tea was offered.

The manager considered. He was relatively new to Mussoorie, so he thought it best to call for the front office manager.

"Samir, do you know of a house called Pine Woods Estate?" The manager asked.

"No, sir. I have not heard of a house by that name in Mussoorie."

"Perhaps the name has changed," said the manager. Turning to Sir Henry, he asked, "Why do you wish to know about this house?"

"My family used to live in Mussoorie many years ago," said Henry.

"I see. Then perhaps you should visit the Mussoorie Library. They may have some old maps there, or maybe there is a person who knows about the old days," the manager suggested.

Henry thanked him and left with Mary. Soon afterwards, the two walked down the steep slope from the Lexton Plaza Hotel to the library.

The librarian, a cheerful middle-aged lady dressed in a bright red salwar-kameez, was very helpful after Henry explained what he was looking for. She was unable to identify Pine Woods Estate but gave the couple some old maps to look at, which they both struggled with—the fine lettering not helping their cause. The librarian kept up a friendly chatter as the two tried to locate the house on the maps.

"Don't you know anything about the house at all?" the librarian asked.

Henry thought for a while and replied, "Is there a graveyard in Mussoorie?"

"Yes, there are two. One on Camel's Back Road and the other in Landour. Why do you ask?"

"There is a legend in our family that we used to live in a ghostly house," said Henry with a laugh. "So, I thought that perhaps the house may be next to a graveyard or something like that."

"I don't think the Landour graveyard has any houses right next to it. So, maybe what you are looking for is the one on Camel's Back Road," the librarian concluded.

"How many houses can be found close to the graveyard?" Mary asked eagerly.

"I can think of three," said the librarian after giving it some thought.

"What are their names?" Mary asked.

"The three are Ida Villa, Hydrangea Bank and Nautiyal Cottage." The librarian gave them directions for the graveyard, and the couple was immediately off to Camel's Back Road.

The road was unpaved, and the only traffic comprised horses and a few pedestrians. The views were breathtaking, with the snow-capped peaks gleaming in all their radiant glory. Henry and Mary reached the gate of the graveyard and asked a passer-by for directions. He gestured towards a path leading up, so they walked up to find the gate of Hydrangea Bank to their left. It was broken and swung slowly on its hinges. They walked in and climbed to the house. It was derelict, with the roof having fallen in at some places and the windowpanes broken.

At the back of the house, they finally found a man who came out on hearing their voices. He spoke a little English and he told them that the last English owners were called Taverner, and they had left in the 1940s. After that, the house had remained vacant and gradually gone to seed. He showed them the way to Ida Villa, and they walked towards it.

There was a boy playing on the terrace.

"Is this Ida Villa?" Mary asked.

"Yes," said the boy.

"May we come in please?" Henry asked.

"Yes," said the boy. He opened the little gate and let them in. They followed him to the front door, where they found a man standing.

"Good morning, what may I do for you?" the man asked.

"Good morning. I am Henry Tavistock and this is my wife, Mary. We are from England."

"Do come in. I am Dr Mathur, and this is my nephew Nanhe."

They sat down on the old cane sofas in the drawing room. Nanhe went to ask for some tea.

"We are sorry to barge in like this, but we are looking for an old house called Pine Woods Estate," said Henry.

"I see. I can't recall a house by that name around here," said Dr Mathur.

Henry told him a part of the story. Dr Mathur was intrigued. "Well, you know, it can't be either Ida Villa or Hydrangea Bank as these houses only came up in the twentieth century. So, that leaves only the cottage near the Parsi graveyard gate."

The Tavistocks got up to take their leave.

"I wish you luck on your quest. Do let me know if you finally find the estate that you are looking for," said Dr Mathur.

They were fairly tired by now. They had been walking around for almost three hours, and it was nearing lunchtime. They were undecided on whether to walk into yet another house.

"Now that we've come so far, let's just give it a go, I guess," said Mary a little dispiritedly.

They walked down the road from Ida Villa. Just next to the Parsi graveyard gate, there was a little path leading down to Nautiyal Cottage. It was a small house on a steep slope, so it was built on stilts. The graveyard was right next to it, quiet in the afternoon sun. The graves gleamed as the dappled sunlight fell on them. A chill ran down Mary's spine.

"I think I can breathe in the ghostliness of the house," said Mary.

The cottage was quite rundown. The broken stairs with no handrails led to a little concrete bridge over a gap between the hillside and the house. The roof was badly in need of paint and moss grew in unsightly patches on the walls. The plaster was broken at many places. Clearly, the inhabitants of Nautiyal Cottage had fallen on hard times.

Henry knocked on the faded green door. After a wait, it was opened by a man roughly the same height and build as him. He looked inquiringly at the visitors and asked, "What do you want?"

"We are from England. We are looking for a house called Pine Woods Estate," said Henry.

The man looked at Henry with an odd expression on his face. He said, "You had better come in."

He stepped aside and they entered the house. The sitting room was untidy with many things scattered around. The man cleared up some space on a sofa and gestured for them to sit.

He then called to someone in the next room. "Dadi, Mama, they have come."

It was a somewhat odd thing to say, and Henry and Mary exchanged glances. They did not have to wait for long.

A middle-aged lady pushing a wheelchair entered the room. Henry and Mary stood up as they entered. There was an awkward silence.

The wizened old lady sitting in the wheelchair finally spoke in English. "My grandmother always said you would come one day, and that is what I told my children too." She continued after a pause, "What is your name?"

"I am Henry Tavistock and this is my wife, Mary."

"Henry Tavistock! What do you want from us?" the old lady asked.

"We are actually looking for a house called Pine Woods Estate," said Henry. He could not make out whether the old lady was hostile. There was an undercurrent in the room that he could not quite fathom.

"Kamala, could you please get the painting," said the old lady abruptly. There was a strained silence after her peremptory command.

The middle-aged woman left the room. She returned soon with a large oil painting mounted in an ornate, old-fashioned, gilt frame. She placed it on the ground against a cupboard so that they could all see it.

The painting was made in early Victorian style. It showed a man standing next to his seated wife.

"This is Henry Tavistock," said the old lady. "He was my grandfather."

There was a long silence as the group absorbed the impact of what she had said. Henry got up to examine the painting more closely. The man was dressed in a frock coat and had a trimmed beard. The woman was wearing a gown with her hair up. She was depicted as being darker than her husband but not noticeably so. She looked very beautiful.

"He just left one day and took one son with him," said the old lady.

"He had more children?" Henry asked. "I did not know that."

"How should you know? He had forgotten about his Indian family. Yes, he had another son called Anand. He was my father," the bitterness in her voice evident. "My grandmother reverted to her maiden name after he left. We have always been Nautiyals after that."

"Henry Tavistock had a bad time after he returned to England," said Henry suddenly.

"He was being punished for his sins," said Kamala fiercely. The old lady shushed her.

"What happened to him?" The old lady was now curious.

"His son by his English wife was a dissolute character. He died young and his wife soon followed. My ancestor is Robert, his son from his Indian wife. I know her name was Basanti," said Henry.

"So, you are our relative!" The old lady exclaimed. "My name is Basanti too. I was named after her."

In some strange way, the atmosphere in the room lightened with her words.

"Robert went to South Africa and made a very large fortune there. Later, he was made a baronet," said Henry. "He remembered very little about India and never mentioned that he had a brother, but he did recall that their house was called Pine Woods Estate and that it was in Mussoorie where Henry Tavistock spent a large part of his time. All these were just stories for us passed down from one generation to the next. There was nothing written down."

"But what made you come to India? Why now, after so many years?" Basanti asked.

"He has always been obsessed with his family's history," said Mary. "It was I who persuaded him to come here and look for his roots. We thought we were looking for a house. Little did we know that we would find his family here." Her eyes were brimming with emotion, and she held her husband's hand tightly as she spoke.

"Let's have lunch," said Basanti. She overruled Henry's feeble attempts to leave and soon lunch was served. The dining table was too small to hold all of them, so they served themselves and ate buffet style. Henry and Mary were not used to Indian food, but the warmth and hospitality of the Indian family was overwhelming.

"Was this house called Pine Woods Estate earlier?" Henry asked.

"No, no! Pine Woods House was a very large bungalow built on the estate. My grandmother had to sell it and some of our land as the family's fortunes went down after Henry left. This cottage was built later," said Basanti. "We have been just managing since then." She pointed to another house a little further away through the window. "That was Pine Woods House, though it was renamed by the new owners."

By the time lunch was over, Henry had taken many photographs with his Kodak camera. Addressing him, Basanti said, "Before you leave, there is a letter that I would like to show you. It was written by my grandmother to me as my parents had died earlier. She was old by then and wanted me to know the family history." She took out some papers from her purse and began to read aloud. The letter was written on old paper, in Hindi. "I will read out an English translation that I worked on by myself."

Mussoorie

12 July 1888

Dearest Basanti,

You are, as yet, too young to understand what I want to say to you. I am old now but once I was young and beautiful, and foolish too! My father, Banwari Lal, was a very respected man. When he learnt that I had fallen in love with a gora saheb, he was horrified. It was against our traditions. What made it worse was that he was a married man and had a son. But I was adamant. Now when I think back on it, it doesn't seem that Henry really wanted to get married. He just wanted to satisfy his lust, but I was too young to know the ways of men. When my father insisted on marriage, Henry gave in. He married me and I was overjoyed. It was an idyllic time at first. He taught me English, and I started to wear English clothes and even imagined myself as a gora memsaheb! How foolish I was. Pine Woods House had been almost fully constructed, but it needed to be furnished. I did not know then that Henry had taken huge debts to finance the construction and furnishings. The debts were a curse that almost buried us after he left.

His British colleagues and friends frowned on him. Such a marriage was an abomination in their eyes. It became worse after 1857 when the days of the Company came to an end. Now, we were under the direct rule of Malika Victoria, and the British were more domineering than ever before. Henry insisted on baptising my elder son, whom he had named Robert, but I refused to let him take my Anand to the church.

He just left one day. Obviously, he had been planning to leave for a while, evading all his responsibilities towards his family—it was also to get away from repaying the debts. He took my beloved firstborn with him, and I never saw them again.

There was a dead silence in the room as Basanti read out the letter. Henry sat with downcast eyes as if the perfidy of his ancestor was his responsibility. Mary sat close to him, trying to console him with her warmth. After a pause, Basanti resumed reading:

Things began to fall apart almost immediately. Henry's creditors, who had been patiently waiting for the gora saheb to settle their bills, were not so forbearing now. There was a lot of pressure on me. My father was helpful, but even his business had got impacted as the British took umbrage to the fact that his daughter had married an Englishman. I had no money and nobody to help me. Finally, when I could not withstand it any more, I sold Pine Woods House and most of the land. We moved to my father's house while Nautiyal Cottage was being built—a far cry from the false grandeur of my youth!

Luckily, the American school that had recently opened in Mussoorie agreed to admit Anand. Since then, all my children and grandchildren have had an English education. That is perhaps the only gift that Henry left for us.

You may think that I lived and died a bitter old woman. That is not so. My life has been through many ups and downs, but I have no bitterness in me. Henry must have had his own compulsions for what he did. He was unjust not only to me but also to his first wife and their child. I do not have the large-heartedness to forgive him, but our children are not to blame for what he did.

One day, an Englishman will come looking for us. He will also be my flesh and blood. Embrace him and let the balm of forgiveness wash over our family.

Basanti Nautiyal

7

Craig's Heights

The house was perched on a little spur on the right as you climbed the steep path from the graveyard on Camel's Back Road to Gun Hill. It lived up to its name when gusts of wind swirled around just prior to the monsoon season. The wind howled during the day as the storm built up in the afternoon. The tin roof rattled fiercely, and it seemed to be in acute danger of being blown away. Perchance, if a door had been left open, it banged hard and often the glass panes would shatter. It was a dramatic location, showcasing the untrammelled power of nature.

For some reason, the winds were always still on a full moon night as if in deference to a greater power. The moonlight glinted on the Himalayan oak trees and shone on the black and white tiled floor in the veranda. It was eerily quiet on such a night as the slightest sound got magnified and echoed off the distant mountains.

Rakesh woke up with a start. The moonlight was streaming in through the half-open window and fell directly on his bed. It was a warm night, and he had felt uncomfortably hot under the heavy quilt. He had thrown it off and had fallen into an uneasy sleep around 10.30.

The luminous dial of his watch showed that the time was just after midnight. A dog was howling in the distance. An eerie sound that went on and on. But it was not the dog that had wakened him. Somewhere in the house, a door shut. It was a stealthy, furtive sound as if somebody wanted to conceal what they were doing. Perhaps someone had gone to the bathroom, he imagined. With a sigh, he turned over and went back to sleep.

The morning was fresh and dewy. It was a warm, clear day and the cobwebs of the night seemed like a chimera in the dazzling sunshine. Rakesh dressed and came down for breakfast. He had taken up a room in Craig's Heights as a paying guest. He was studying for the IAS exam and needed a quiet place where he would not be disturbed for a month. The house seemed perfect for his needs when he had responded to a classified advertisement in the Delhi edition of the *Daily Clarion*.

His parents thought it was a quixotic thing to do. They had wanted him to enrol in a coaching class in Delhi, which seemed logical as that would have been close to home, but he was adamant that he could make it on his own. He was a brilliant student and a good athlete, especially in the long-distance races. He was a loner though, an introvert who liked silences and his own company. Perhaps it was this that had brought him to Mussoorie.

It was early in the season and the tourist hordes had not yet descended on the quiet hill station. He had arrived a week ago and had made his way from Picture Palace with a coolie to carry his baggage. The steep climb to his chosen home did not deter him and he found the view splendid. The weather had been clement, and he had enjoyed the brilliant sunshine on the terrace as he read the history tomes that were to be his companions for the exam. He had been greeted by an old servant who seemed to be the general factotum for the house. He had been a little surprised to discover that he was the only guest. Maybe the house would fill up later in the season.

That day, the heat seemed to build up unbearably. Lunch was a listless affair, and he resolved to go out for dinner to one of the restaurants on the Mall Road. He told the old servant, when he met him for lunch, and was heard out with an impassive expression. He went out in the garden after lunch to find that a fresh breeze had sprung up. Clouds were building up in the valleys and soon the sky was overcast. It was one of the dramatic changes of weather that often happen in the hills. By teatime, the rain had started in earnest and Rakesh found himself marooned inside the house. When the old servant brought his tea, he had to shamefacedly tell him that his plans for going out had to be cancelled. The servant received the news with the same impassive countenance and soon left the room, leaving Rakesh to his own devices. The evening stretched interminably ahead, so he decided to explore the house.

There was a wooden staircase with two arms leading up to a landing on the first floor. The guest wing was to the left. It had four rooms, three of which were empty. There was a heavy wooden door on the other side with a brass handle. He tried it tentatively and to his surprise it opened soundlessly as if the hinges had been greased recently. He went through and found himself in a dimly lit, narrow corridor. It was carpeted, so his soft canvas shoes made no sound as he walked in carefully. Just then, a door at the far end opened and the old servant came out. He saw Rakesh and gestured for him to go back.

Embarrassed at being caught out, Rakesh backed away. The door to the corridor shut with a soft thud. The sound was somehow familiar. He waited for the old servant to come out to apologise, but the servant did not appear for some time, so Rakesh went back to his room. The little incident had left him more shaken than he thought. He sat down on the bed and may have dozed off. He awoke with a start to find the room in darkness. There was a soft knock on the door that had woken him up. Rubbing the sleep from his eyes, he walked to the door and opened it. The old servant was standing outside holding a candlestick.

"Dinner is ready."

Rakesh cleared his throat and asked, "Has the electricity gone?"

"Yes," said the old servant. "It has been gone for quite a while."

Rakesh nodded. "I will be down right away."

He went back into his room, washed his face and straightened his clothes. He came down the staircase and took his place at the dining table. There were two more places laid for dinner, unusual as no one had joined him for any of the other meals till now. The power supply had not been restored, and the storm was gathering strength.

The wind howled around the house and the windows rattled. The room looked strange and ghostly in the light of the few candles that the old servant had placed on the table. The lights flickered as tendrils of the manic wind found their way into the beleaguered house.

Rakesh felt rather than saw the presence of his dinner companions. Perhaps he had been distracted and missed the moment they had entered; he looked up to see two women approaching the table. He stood up instinctively to greet them. They appeared to be mother and daughter, as they looked rather alike. The older woman was dressed in a black sari while the younger one wore a dark blue salwar-kameez, with her hair up. They took their places at the table. The older woman sat at the head of the table acknowledging his greeting with a slight nod, while the younger one sat opposite Rakesh. No words were spoken. The old servant placed the food on the table. They ate in silence for a while. The rain seemed to have stopped and soon the lights came back on.

Rakesh could see his dinner companions properly for the first time. The older lady must have been very beautiful when she was young. Her perfectly chiselled features and elegant manners were still intact. But Rakesh had eyes only for her daughter. The sudden light flooding the room seemed to have upset her in some way. Her pupils had shrunk to pinpoints and there was an unnatural pallor on her cheeks. As she ate, her teeth gleamed in the light of the chandelier overhead. She was wearing bright red lipstick and there was a dark mole on one cheek. In a strange way, it added to her beauty. She was very attractive in a voluptuous way. Rakesh caught himself staring at her and turned his face away.

Dinner was over and they had moved to the sitting room for coffee when the old woman finally spoke, "Welcome to Craig's Heights. I'm glad you have chosen to stay with us. As you can see, we are very quiet right now."

"Thank you for having me. I was looking for a quiet place for my studies," said Rakesh politely.

"I am Malini Chatterjee, and this is my daughter, Chandni."

The young woman had walked away from the table after dinner. As she walked back to the sitting room, Rakesh watched her moving as if mesmerised. She sat down without saying anything, a little away from her mother.

"It's good to meet you. My name is Rakesh Singh."

The evening ended soon after that with the two women taking their leave. The rain had stopped as the moon had risen. It was a warm night, redolent with the scent of night flowers. Rakesh could see Chandni walking in the garden, and he stood watching her for quite a while. Finally, she went inside.

Still standing at the window, Rakesh decided to go out for a walk. He put on his shoes and let himself out of the front door. He had a set of keys with him, so that he would not need to wake up the household on his return. He walked down the dark path leading to Camel's Back Road and the graveyard below. He turned left at the end of the path on Camel's Back Road and walked along the road with the graveyard below him to the right, silent and quiet in the moonlit night.

He could hear voices in the distance as he walked. There was nervous laughter and the overloud chatter of people who wanted to reassure themselves against the denizens of the night. He met the family near the gate of the Parsi cemetery where the municipality had recently installed a streetlight. They looked at him appraisingly as he went past and finally the man spoke, "Good evening."

Rakesh returned the greeting, and they stopped to talk. It turned out that the middle-aged couple had come over from Delhi with their teenage daughter. They were staying at Craigsville cottages just below Craig's Heights. They were planning to stay in Mussoorie for a fortnight but had been a little taken aback by the loneliness of their surroundings. Rakesh reassured them and they parted with promises to meet again soon. He returned to Craig's Heights much later and let himself in. He went quietly up to his room and softly closed the door. As he was drifting off to sleep, he thought he heard a door shutting somewhere in the house.

Breakfast was late the next day. Rakesh woke up from a deep, almost drugged, sleep at nearly nine o'clock. He dressed and went down to the dining room to find that Malini and Chandni were already there. In the morning sunlight, Chandni looked even more bewitching than at night. Her cheeks seemed to have filled out somehow and her face glowed. She did not speak as they took their places at the dining table. The meal soon ended with some desultory conversation between Malini and Rakesh. He took his leave and went out to the garden to sit under the deodar tree that had become his favourite spot for studying.

It was nearing lunchtime when Rakesh heard the knocking at the front gate. He got up to open it but paused when he saw the old servant walking out of the house towards the gate. He soon returned with a police inspector and constable, who followed him into the house. After almost half an hour, the old servant came out and gestured to Rakesh to come with him. He entered the house to see the two policemen sitting on a sofa with Malini sitting on a chair opposite them. He sat down on a chair next to her.

The inspector spoke, "Is your name Rakesh Singh?" The question was asked in an official tone. Rakesh nodded. "And you are staying here as a paying guest?"

"Yes," said Rakesh.

"Did you go out last night?" the inspector asked.

"Yes, I did, but what is this about?"

"I am the one asking questions," the inspector reminded him authoritatively. "Did you meet anyone when you were out?"

Rakesh told the inspector about his meeting with the family on Camel's Back Road.

"Did you walk further?" the inspector inquired.

"Yes, as a matter of fact, I did. It was a fine night after the storm and I walked all the way around Camel's Back Road to the Mall on the library side and then came up from the White Palisades Hotel," said Rakesh. "Why are you asking me these questions?"

The inspector relented. "A teenage girl is missing. She is the daughter of the family living in the Craigsville cottages. The parents had a cottage to themselves while the girl was staying in another one close by. She was not found in the morning, so the parents have called the police."

"Maybe she has gone out for a walk on her own," Malini chimed in.

"Several hours have passed since she was reported missing. She would have come back by now. Is there anyone else in the house?" the inspector queried.

For some reason, Malini appeared to hesitate. Finally, she spoke, "My daughter is here. She is resting."

The inspector looked a little uncomfortable. After a long pause, he spoke firmly, "I need to speak with her directly."

Rakesh got the impression that he was concealing something.

"I will ask her to come down," said Malini. "She is not keeping well, and I would request you not to be harsh with her."

She left the room and returned with Chandni who looked as if she had just woken up from a deep sleep. Her eyes were vacant, and her hair was dishevelled. Her mother was holding her arm tightly and they came and stood in front of the inspector.

"Did you go out last night?" the inspector asked.

Chandni did not say anything, so the inspector repeated his question. This time, Chandni shook her head and said, "No." Her voice was gruff and unexpected coming from a beautiful girl like her. It was the first time that Rakesh had heard her speak. He was astounded by the change that had come about her since they had met at breakfast.

The inspector looked as if he would have liked to ask more questions, but he finally put away his pen in his breast pocket and shut his notebook. He took his leave after inquiring about the other houses in the vicinity. As it turned out, most of them were still unoccupied as it was early in the season.

The torn and mutilated body of the teenage girl was found in the ravines below Antariksh Bhawan on Camel's Back Road the day after she disappeared from Craigsville. Her body appeared to have been drained of blood and her torso and vagina had been brutally ripped. She had probably been attacked by wild pigs who had gnawed off her neck, such that her head had separated from the body. They had also gored her abdomen and chewed her arms and legs. It was a grisly sight even for the police and medical staff. The autopsy was inconclusive, as it was not possible to establish whether death had been caused by an accidental fall after being attacked by the pigs or had she been killed and her body thrown into the ravines where the pigs had gored her. The time of death was also uncertain other than the likelihood that she had died on the same night she had disappeared.

The inspector visited Craig's Heights again that day. He sternly bade them all to remain in Mussoorie till the investigation was complete. He conveyed the same message to all the residents of the other houses around. The girl's funeral was held the next day with the body being completely wrapped in a winding sheet. Many people came to mourn, and the hill station was thrown into a pall of gloom. The police investigation continued but no breakthrough came their way.

Rakesh asked the inspector if he could leave for Delhi. A week later, his request was granted once he gave his address and contact references in Delhi. He left Mussoorie the same afternoon after bidding goodbye to his hosts. He told Malini that he had been quite shaken by what had happened and wanted some time away from Mussoorie. He said that he would return after a week, so he was leaving his luggage behind. He had cut his visit short but who could blame him after what had happened?

It was late afternoon by the time he came to the Picture Palace bus stand. He had wrapped a muffler around his head and was wearing a cap as the evening had turned chilly; he bought a ticket from the conductor, who barely glanced at him. The bus was full already by the time Rakesh got inside so he had to remain standing, along with a few others. He was standing very close to the door when the bus started its journey to Dehradun. Soon afterwards, the bus stopped at Kin Craig as some more people wanted to get in. A few people got off too.

The gate opened silently with the duplicate key that had been made recently. A shadowy figure walked noiselessly to the back of the house and let himself in. A windowpane had been dislodged in the bathroom; he put his hand in stealthily and turned the latch. Once inside the bathroom, he opened the door a crack as he could hear some voices.

"I thought she was improving but she seems to have regressed," said Malini.

"That often happens. All that we can hope for is to continue with the treatment," said a male voice. "Her mental illness cannot be cured. It can only be alleviated."

"Thank you, Doctor," said Malini.

He could hear footsteps leading to the front door. Shortly afterwards, the light was switched off and he could hear the footsteps going upstairs. He waited for a long time in the study adjoining the bathroom he had come in from. The house settled down and finally slept. He crept upstairs and went into the third room on the right where the girl slept. The door was locked but he had a key. It turned soundlessly and he went inside like a ghost. He had the chloroform in his pocket and the girl was soon unconscious.

Much later, he stole down the stairs and let himself out from the bathroom the way he had come. He caught the last bus to Delhi that left at eleven o'clock from Mussoorie Library. He was wearing dark trousers with a sweater to keep the cold away. With the cap and muffler wrapped around his neck, he looked quite unrecognisable.

Rakesh was adept at covering his tracks.

8

Ivy Cottage

The eponymously named Ivy Cottage stood in a little garden of its own just below the Mall Road. The ivy growing on its walls was carefully trimmed, leaving place for the green-frame windows and the front door. There was a little gravel path that led to the cottage from the road going down to the Regency Park School. Passing through a honeysuckle arch with a neatly trimmed lawn bordered by hollyhocks and dahlias, you would see a green-painted door with a brass knocker. Once inside, the sense of perfect taste and manicured elegance continued. The sitting room was upholstered in chintz, leading to a small dining space beyond. The kitchen was at the back and a path through the kitchen garden led to the servants' quarters. There were two bedrooms upstairs and a small study lined with books—the perfect retreat for a cultivated mind.

Vijay Chandra, for he was the fortunate owner of Ivy Cottage, lived alone apart from a discreet manservant appropriately and inevitably named Ram Singh. They had apparently served in the army together where Ram Singh had saved his future master's life, according to the more gullible gossipmongers of the town. Mr Chandra was a tall, lean, dark man. He was always immaculately dressed, favouring tweed coats and flannel trousers while promenading on the Mall Road. He invariably spent almost six months every year in Mussoorie. Nobody quite knew where he came from as his name was intriguingly indeterminate and did not reveal his antecedents quite as clearly as names often do in India. He was obviously wealthy, but again, nobody knew what he did for a living.

"I'm desperate," said Deepti. She had walked into Ivy Cottage one afternoon when her husband was playing bridge with his friends at the White Palisades Hotel.

Vijay took her in his arms and said caressingly, "What has happened?"

"He's asked for money again!"

"I thought you had paid him only a month ago."

"Yes, but his letter arrived this morning." Deepti looked distraught and tearful, but nothing could disguise the classical beauty of her face or the sensuousness of her lithe figure. "I look at all the mail that arrives first as I am scared that Ashok will find one of these letters. See, this is what I found today morning."

She held out a plain, yellow-coloured envelope. Her name was typed on the cover and the letter was typed too. He did not take it and waited for her to open it and read out the contents. They were simple enough. The unknown writer demanded another Rs 10,000. There was no threat, but the implication was clear enough. He had given Deepti positive proof of her infidelity earlier with a promise that if she paid once, he would not trouble her again. The hollowness of the promise had been amply proven several times over.

"Well, Ashok is rich enough. He's unlikely to notice another Rs 10,000 gone from his bank account," said Vijay a shade flippantly.

Deepti looked at him reproachfully. "It's not just the money," she said tearfully.

"I didn't mean that," said Vijay instantly.

"Maybe I should tell Ashok everything," said Deepti.

"What will you tell him? That you have been having an affair with me for the past three years. No, no, he will never forgive you," said Vijay.

He spent the rest of the afternoon soothing her fears and apprehensions, as he was most adept at doing. She left before five o'clock to stroll over to the White Palisades Hotel to join her husband for the evening promenade on the Mall Road.

Ashok Goenka was a tall, powerfully built man with a craggy face. His hair was long and wavy and there was a certain ruthlessness about the curve of his jaw. He was, as always, carelessly dressed, with an old pullover thrown over an ancient pair of jeans. He violated the dress code of the hotel every time he walked into the bar, but nobody had the guts to tell him so. The bridge game was just ending when Deepti walked in. Ashok's friends greeted her hurriedly but left without lingering to talk to the couple. They walked out of the hotel with a nod to the hovering waiter who took it to mean that the bill for all the tea, coffee and snacks should be added to Ashok's account as usual. The waiter ushered them out and held the door open as they went past.

They looked every inch a beautiful couple as they strolled on the Mall Road. When Deepti's father, one of the richest Marwari businessmen in India, had fixed the marriage of his only daughter to Ashok, it came as a bit of a surprise in business circles. Ashok, though of the right lineage, was just starting off in life after his family had suffered a series of setbacks. They were no match for Deepti's family, and these things mattered in Marwari circles. Perhaps he had the foresight to see what Ashok was capable of for Ashok grew from strength to strength.

In a very short period, he could be counted amongst the most promising upcoming businessmen in the country. His ability to handle the all-powerful government and get concessions and benefits for himself was unrivalled as was his financial acumen. Having a powerful father-in-law obviously helped.

Deepti discovered early in her marriage that it was only a marriage of convenience. For Ashok, gaining her father's goodwill was more important than Deepti's feelings. It was a loveless marriage and a childless one too. Surrounded by luxury, she was the proverbial canary in a gilded cage. Deepti's father had been in the habit of coming to Mussoorie every year till his health failed him. Ashok and Deepti also came up a few times, but Ashok found the hill station too constricting. He continued to come for short periods but for the most part, Deepti would stay on her own. Her father's estate was one of the most impressive in Mussoorie and the old servants had seen her grow up from childhood.

Three years ago, she had met Vijay Chandra. It was at a party hosted by one of Deepti's friends from Bombay at the Lexton Plaza Hotel. Vijay was a bachelor and Deepti was alone too, so it was inevitable that the two would be thrown together. Vijay's attentiveness, care and concern was a welcome change from the brusque behaviour of her husband.

She was putty in the hands of the seasoned womaniser.

The first letter had arrived soon afterwards. The yellow envelope that was to become all too familiar was handed over to Deepti by a manservant as she came down for lunch. She opened it and struggled to breathe as she read it.

> My dear Mrs Goenka,
>
> How are the afternoons at Ivy Cottage? So much love should be shared with your husband, don't you think? I am a poor man, and I need a little something to keep quiet. Rs 10,000 in cash. Day after tomorrow. Keep the money in a brown paper bag. Walk up to the chhattri on Camel's Back Road at exactly 2.00 p.m. Sit inside. Make sure that there is nobody else around, I will be watching. Leave the bag and walk away towards Mussorie Library. That's all. Just do this and I will never trouble you again.
>
> One who knows.
>
> PS—I hope you like the photograph.

The photograph made her stomach churn. She had gone on a picnic towards Benog with Vijay, and they had walked down a secluded path where Vijay had laid out a picnic lunch. Later, they had made love on the rug. Someone had obviously followed them, as the photograph was clear and explicit.

She had immediately left for Ivy Cottage.

"Look at this," she said as she rushed into the cottage and thrust the letter and photograph into Vijay's hands.

He read them carefully and handed them back to her.

"Looks like this scoundrel has the goods on you," said Vijay.

"What should I do?" Deepti was close to tears.

"I think you will have to pay him what he wants," said Vijay. "If he goes to Ashok, the fat will be in the fire."

They discussed what to do. Afterwards, Deepti went by herself to the First Bank of India and withdrew money from her account in Mussoorie. The manager was deferential, even though the account did not have enough money in it. He accepted the cheque drawn on her account in Bombay and handed her the cash in crisp hundred-rupee notes after a brief wait. The visit to the chhattri was nerve-wracking. Vijay had told her that she must go alone as the blackmailer may get alarmed if she was with someone. Eventually, it turned out to be quite easy. There was nobody around and she just left the brown paper packet on the bench and walked away. She did not see anyone and did not look back.

"I'm thinking of leaving Ashok," said Deepti one afternoon as they lay in their bed in Ivy Cottage. She got up and went to the window.

"Hmm. Come back to bed, darling," said Vijay.

"Be serious, Vijay. I'm not being fair to him. He may be inattentive, but he's not a bad person," said Deepti.

Vijay thought about Ashok and his reputation. He had had a string of girlfriends before he got married and very little had changed afterwards. Proverbially, his wife would be the last to know.

Vijay had received a little note hand-delivered to his guest house room in Churchgate two years ago. It was December, so the Bombay weather was balmy, quite unlike Mussoorie that would have been very cold at this time.

The note was very short. It was typewritten. It said simply:

> 10.12.63
>
> Dear Mr Chandra,
>
> Kindly make it convenient to come to my office tomorrow (Wednesday, 11 December) at 11 a.m.
>
> Ashok Goenka

The address, a building on Pherozeshah Mehta Road, was printed on the letterhead. The signature was a bold scrawl. Vijay broke out into a cold sweat as he read and reread the simple and arrogant message. He had no idea about how Ashok knew that he was in Bombay and where he was staying. The prospect of a pleasurable evening with a delightfully forward socialite much given to air kisses and calling everyone "daahling" was rather dashed. He called and cancelled their engagement. He considered calling Deepti but decided against it. He had met Ashok socially in Mussoorie and had felt the raw power of the man. The meeting tomorrow was going to be tricky. He wondered why he had been summoned in such an abrupt fashion.

The old but well-maintained elevator looked like a cage. A wide wooden staircase was wrapped around it, and he saw busy executives scurrying up and down as the elevator slowly ascended to the fifth floor which was also the top floor of the building owned by Ashok's company. Dressed in a white uniform, the ancient servitor who operated the lift did not stop at any of the intermediate floors after he learnt that Vijay had a meeting with the chairman.

Vijay was sweating profusely in his formal suit despite the relatively cooler weather. There was only one office on the fifth floor. Vijay entered a wood-panelled waiting area to be greeted by Ashok's secretary, Janet. She went inside to inform Ashok about his arrival and soon, Vijay was ushered into a vast office with windows overlooking the busy street below. Ashok was standing near his desk, looking out of the window as Vijay came in. Janet closed the door behind her, leaving the two men alone. Unsure of what he should do, Vijay remained standing till Ashok turned around. He was dressed in casual clothes as usual and sat down on his chair behind the desk.

"So, Mr Casanova, what brings you to Bombay," said Ashok in a gravelly voice. He obviously did not expect an answer as he reached down and took out a large yellow envelope from the drawer by the side of his desk. Opening it, he reached inside and took out a glossy photo that he pushed across the table to Vijay. Vijay took it and found himself looking down at the same photo that Deepti had showed him that summer.

"Well?" Ashok said. He was lounging in his chair, totally at ease.

"I'm sorry," said Vijay hesitantly.

"Shut up, you motherfucker," barked Ashok. He was still lounging in his chair but there was a menacing gleam in his eyes. He reached into the yellow envelope again and took out another photo that he also slid across the table. Vijay paled. It was a perfectly clear photo of him picking up a brown paper bag from the chhattri on Camel's Back Road.

"The manager of the First Bank of India in Mussoorie had put an urgent call to me before he handed over the notes to Deepti. The notes were marked, and the police have proof that you have spent them at various places in Mussoorie," said Ashok. He smiled maliciously as he spoke.

"What do you want from me?" Vijay asked. His face was ashen and he was finding it difficult to breathe.

"Nothing," said Ashok. He got up languidly and walked across to a cabinet on the wall at the side of the office. "Drink?" He took out a bottle and two crystal glasses and poured out two stiff drinks. Vijay got up and picked up one of the glasses. He drank almost all the whisky in one gulp before looking up at Ashok.

"What do you mean?" Vijay said, summoning his strength.

"Precisely what I said. Nothing," said Ashok as he sipped the whisky appreciatively.

"I will stop seeing Deepti," said Vijay.

"That's not what I said," said Ashok. "You have obviously got a neat little modus operandi going. Seduce rich women and then blackmail them. They are too scared to tell anyone, so you can milk the pigeon till it bleeds." He was obviously enjoying himself at the expense of the tawdry blackmailer.

"Please tell me what I should do. I will do anything, anything you want," said Vijay, almost wringing his hands. "How did you get hold of the photograph?"

"Oh, that one of you and your *inamorata in flagrante delicto*?" Ashok said.

Vijay nodded.

"Your photographer is a pliable man," said Ashok with a laugh.

"Please, please tell me what to do!" Vijay said, now wringing his hands.

"I have already told you. Just continue with the good work. Enjoy your steamy afternoons at Ivy Cottage but don't show your face in Bombay again. You can milk your pigeons for all I care but make sure you don't kill the goose that lays the golden eggs. Be reasonable and discreet, and all will be well," said Ashok nonchalantly, happily mixing metaphors.

"You don't want me to stop seeing Deepti?" Vijay said incredulously.

"How many times must I tell you, bloody fool. Now get out of my office. Your luggage will be packed when you get back to the guest house and a ticket to Dehradun will be lying at the reception. Get OUT!" The menace and command in Ashok's voice was unmistakeable. Vijay got up and stumbled out of the office.

Ashok's expression changed after Vijay had left the room. He walked up to the bar cabinet and poured himself another drink as he recalled the difficulties of the last year. His business was based on leveraging other people's money, and it was unravelling. Left with no option before his creditors closed on him, he had sought an audience with Seth Dhanraj, Deepti's father.

Seth-ji's magnificent bungalow, Ashiana, was located on Worli Sea Face. Ashok was ushered into a book-lined study on the ground floor that was dominated by a large teak desk with an old-fashioned revolving cane chair. Seth-ji walked in after almost ten minutes, dressed in his traditional dhoti and starched kurta. He shook hands with Ashok and sat down on the revolving chair. He took off his gold-rimmed glasses, wiped them with a handkerchief and put them back on.

"I wanted to meet you, sir," said Ashok.

"That is evident." His daughter Deepti had shared the difficulties that she had been facing with Ashok, but he had refrained from interfering.

"I need some money." Ashok did not waste any time in coming to the point.

"That is also evident," Seth-ji responded dryly.

"It's only temporary." Ashok spent the next ten minutes explaining what had happened and why he was confident that he would be able to recover shortly.

Seth-ji listened with an inscrutable expression on his face. He had already commissioned a full investigation into Ashok's affairs and knew more than Ashok was prepared to tell him. He waited patiently for Ashok to finish.

"I see that Deepti has gone back to Mussoorie," said Seth-ji.

The remark was unexpected, coming as it did after Ashok had finished talking about his business. He was intelligent enough to understand the import of the statement.

"I am concerned about my daughter," Seth-ji added bluntly. "I am prepared to bail you out, but you must ensure that she is happy and that your marriage works. There is no room for divorce in our family." The threat was unmistakeable.

Ashok nodded and rose to take his leave. The interview was over.

It was in Mussoorie that year that Ashok heard some murmurs about the goings-on at Ivy Cottage. After that, it was a simple matter for Mark, his trusted Anglo-Indian butler who had been his classmate in school and inseparable thereafter, to find the photographer whom Vijay had hired. Mussoorie was a small place with not too many photographers and Vijay had made the mistake of assuming that his money would result in a permanent gag on his accomplice, especially one who needed money to feed his drinking and gambling habits. As it happened, Mark had hired the photographer for many photo shoots for the society papers for Ashok and Deepti earlier and had flagged him as a person who would not be averse to bending a few rules.

"This looks like proof positive," Ashok remarked.

"Yes sir. The photo can be used as grounds for divorce."

"But I don't want a divorce."

"Well then, it can also be used to ensure that your wife does not file for divorce."

"Explain."

"It's simple. We know that Vijay is blackmailing Deepti. We must ensure that he keeps doing it but at a level that does not panic Deepti. She will be so guilty that she won't contemplate going for a divorce knowing that all her skeletons may tumble out of the closet. As for Vijay, he knows that his gravy train may get derailed if he overplays his hand. On the other hand, it can continue indefinitely if he handles it well, which he is certainly capable of doing." explained Mark.

Ashok sat in silence for a long time mulling over Mark's words.

"You know, that is an absolutely brilliant idea! We shall do exactly that," exclaimed Ashok as he got up and vigorously shook his counsellor's hand.

9

Leopard's Face

The oddly named house, Leopard's Face, was more of a description of the shape of the hill rather than the house itself. There was no drama about the house. Just an old colonial bungalow with a faded red tin roof with rust patches on it and walls that had once been painted white. It was situated at the extreme end of the cart road from Mussoorie Library that goes all the way around Vincent Hill. It was an isolated location as the road was little used.

The house was owned by Colonel Debenham in British times. He had retired in the 1940s and had decided to settle down in Mussoorie, which he loved, rather than going back to the dreary fogs of London. His wife, Emily, was an enthusiastic hostess and the house was full of laughter and gaiety in those days. The Debenhams had three daughters, all beautiful and charming, so the road to Leopard's Face was full of aspiring beaus; and soon enough, the two younger girls were betrothed and married shortly thereafter at Christ Church.

They left with their husbands for England leaving their eldest sister, Dorothy, a prey to doubt and confusion about why she had not been chosen as well. Her parents consoled her and continued with their merry lifestyle in the hope that she would also find a groom sooner rather than later. There were beaus aplenty in the war years, with army officers resting and recuperating in Mussoorie from the Eastern theatres of war. Dorothy recovered her spirits and fell in love with an obliging captain. They were engaged quickly and for a moment, there seemed to be no impediment to her happiness.

The captain had to go back to South-east Asia when his leave was over and he left Dorothy behind, secure in her happiness. Alas, the astute captain did not survive the war. His was not a heroic death, unfortunately, as he succumbed to malaria during the operations in Malaya. The war was to end soon afterwards but he did not return, leaving Dorothy bereft of her slender chance of conjugal happiness.

Life at Leopard's Face continued apace. India became independent and slowly, the crowd of suitors dwindled to a trickle as the English withdrew to their homeland. Not long thereafter, Emily succumbed to a severe bout of flu and passed away. She was buried in the Camel's Back cemetery. Father and daughter were left as the sole inhabitants of Leopard's Face. The ageing but still sprightly colonel tried valiantly to cling on to the old ways. He maintained an enviable stable and a liveried rickshaw but soon expenses outpaced desire, and the horses had to be sold. The colonel was heartbroken, and his daughter was hard put to console him.

It was a thinly worn facade though, as the very next summer, the colonel found the voluptuous charms of an

Anglo-Indian widow—who had come up to Mussoorie to nurse her ostensibly broken heart—irresistible. Her widow's weeds were soon discarded and the lady whisked away the colonel to a life of comparative luxury in Jhansi where her late husband had left her with a substantial estate. She looked at Dorothy with repugnance and while the colonel remonstrated feebly, his opinions did not count for much. Thus, by the mid-1950s, Dorothy found herself alone in Leopard's Face, facing an uncertain future.

Straitened circumstances are like termites. They eat away at your self-esteem by degrees and very often they are convenient to ignore until the effects are irreversible. The liveried rickshaw was sold and the pullers dismissed. The Debenhams had a family living rent-free in the outhouse and in return the woman cleaned the house and cooked what little food Dorothy needed. It was a beneficial arrangement for all of them, but it was not to last. The woman's husband was lucky to get a government job, and he was soon transferred to a remote corner of Kumaon. They were a childless couple, so the woman decided to move with her husband when he left Mussoorie. The woman made many promises that she would return soon, but the day she left on a warm afternoon in June, Dorothy knew that she would not come back.

It was not possible for her to hire another servant as she could not afford the salary. Thus, Leopard's Face lost another vestige of human habitation and Dorothy the last person whom she could talk to. Admittedly, the conversations were functional, concerned about mundane menus and lamentations about the inexorable increase in the cost of living, but the loss of human contact weighed heavily on the soul. She wrote letters to her sisters and her father but as they began to reflect the desperation of her circumstances, the replies became more infrequent and eventually stopped altogether. Even the solace of a card at Christmas was denied to her.

Dorothy made an effort to walk to Mussoorie Library every day to buy the meagre groceries required to keep body and soul together, but the effort became dreary with repetition. As the seasons followed their inexorable cycle, her visits became more irregular until at times she would not move out of the house for a week. She heard the news of the prime minister's death on her old radio and for a while recalled happier days when she had seen him riding on the Mall Road. They had attended a select party at the Lexton Plaza Hotel where he had made a little speech and Dorothy had been impressed by his erudition. The radio stopped working the very next day as if it had gone into mourning as a harbinger of bad news. She was frantic and took the machine all the way to Landour Bazaar to get it fixed. The mechanic shook his head, talking wisely of valves and pentodes but the upshot was that the cost of repairing the radio was well beyond her means.

Disconsolate, she sold the broken machine to the same mechanic for twenty-five rupees and returned to Leopard's Face without even a voice from the ether left to ameliorate the loneliness of her evenings. That night she opened a bottle of army rum, one of the last left over from the colonel's collection and drank a great deal as the silvery moonlight washed over the bereft house.

At fifty, Dorothy looked older than her years. She had an angular, bony look that had become accentuated as she grew older. Her hair was grey, more pepper than salt, and her few clothes had a worn look. She wore old-fashioned frocks, some of them belonging to her sisters and mother and reminiscent of happier times, but as the days passed by, the effort of washing, drying and ironing them became more and more tedious. She had never been a slovenly woman, but now her clothes had stains on them, and her feet were shod with bathroom slippers from Bata that she had mended herself with a needle and thread from her mother's embroidery box.

There was a little room below the stairs at Leopard's Face. It was a coal cellar as well as a general storeroom. A spade, a rake, garden shears and an untidy mess of garden hoses jostled for space. There was a ladder too and a rope that someone had left there many years ago. Dorothy rarely opened the storeroom. What little cooking she did was on a kerosene stove. The kerosene was filled from a large barrel kept in the kitchen. The kerosene stove had replaced the coal counterpart that had been used in the old days, and with Dorothy's minimal requirements, the kerosene had lasted literally for years. But it had eventually run out and she had to go back to using coal for her cooking.

She entered the crowded store after a long time and filled up a little coal scuttle when a thought came unbidden to her mind.

Never leave a coal fire burning in a closed room, she could hear her mother's voice scolding a hapless servant. *It creates a poisonous gas, and you can die.*

The thought receded but not before she saw the coil of rope lying untidily in the corner. Her father had taught her how to tie a slip knot and the sisters had played cowboy games with a lasso made perhaps with the same rope when they were children. Almost without thinking, she picked up the rope and found herself making a slip knot at the end. She passed the end of the rope through the knot and tested it for strength. It held securely. Then, with a little sigh, she put the rope down, picked up the coal scuttle and left the room.

There is an odd serenity about acceptance. It comes in slow stages, and it is almost imperceptible when realisation dawns at last. It would be wrong to say that Dorothy decided to end her life. She came from a good Christian family and the sheer idea was anathema to her. And yet, the temptation to light a fire and close the windows tightly before sleeping was undeniable. Did she struggle with herself? Perhaps, but who can fathom the still depths of a human mind? She went about her minimal chores with her usual indifference, but increasingly, her thoughts turned towards deliverance and an end to her insufferable existence.

One day in late summer, she was sitting on the front veranda in the morning when she saw a small boy opening the gate. Nobody had entered the house for years. She watched as the little boy came towards her and finally spoke in Hindi.

"Are you a *churail*?" His voice was questioning but unafraid.

Dorothy's Hindi was fluent but slightly accented. "No," she said at last.

"Everyone says you are. You look like one." The unthinking brutality of childhood was evident in the forthright answer.

"Why?" Dorothy asked. It was a long time since she had had a proper conversation with anyone, and her monosyllabic replies were a measure of her hesitation.

"You've got strange hair and your eyes are blue," said the boy emphatically.

Dorothy instinctively ran her hand through her wind-blown, unkempt grey hair.

The boy turned and ran towards the gate. Dorothy got up to stop him but then heard what his youthful ears had picked up before her. The boy's mother was calling him for lunch.

The next day, Dorothy washed her hair. She let it dry in the sun and then combed it in front of a mirror as her mother used to do for her in happier times. She also washed her clothes and tidied the bed. It was extraordinary what a little human contact can do for the soul!

The boy came again and soon his visits became a part of her days that Dorothy really looked forward to. They talked about childish things, and she took out some of the old children's books that were still stored away in a trunk in the box room and began to read to him. He did not understand English well but made rapid progress as the days passed. One day, the boy's mother came to the house as Dorothy was reading to him on the veranda.

"I hope he is not troubling you, memsaheb," the boy's mother said awkwardly.

"No, not at all," Dorothy replied with a smile.

"He is learning a lot from you," said the boy's mother. "I did not realise that he was coming to your house, or I would have stopped him."

"He asked me if I was a churail," said Dorothy.

The boy's mother covered her face with her sari pallu and looked embarrassed. It was evident that she was the originator of this myth. Soon, however, her curiosity overcame her shyness, and she began to ask Dorothy a series of personal questions in typical Indian fashion. The ice was broken.

"You should teach the other children too," said the boy's mother. Rather to her surprise, Dorothy found herself agreeing to the suggestion. As an English child growing up in India, she had lived a segregated life. Her contact with Indian people had been limited to transactional encounters. This was perhaps the first time that an Indian had reached out to her in this way.

Soon afterwards, Dorothy Ma'am's classes started in earnest. Someone suggested that she should get paid for her work and the parents readily agreed. For the first time in many years, Dorothy started seeing some money coming in. It was a welcome, comforting thought. As time went on, Dorothy restarted many of the little things she had lost sight of. The radio made a reappearance and so did the kerosene stove.

One day, while she was cleaning the house, she entered the little storeroom after a long time. While sweeping the floor, her gaze fell on the rope lying untidily in the corner. She bent down, picked it up and deposited it in the kitchen dustbin.

10

Redwood Manor

Redwood Manor did not have any of the giant sequoia trees that grew in California. Perhaps the original owner, an American who taught at Woodstock School, missed the gentle giants of his homeland. He was unmarried and had built the house in the 1920s when he had moved as a Methodist missionary to Mussoorie. He was also perhaps a little presumptuous in naming his house as a manor. It was not big enough or grand enough to be dignified by that epithet.

It was situated below St Paul's Church in a little clearing in the pine forest on the slopes of Lal Tibba, overlooking the Doon Valley. It was a pretty house, designed in the colonial style of the day. What distinguished it were the twin chimneys made in red brick that surmounted the tin roof. In fact, the whole house was built of bricks, a little unusual for the hills. It had the regulation tin roof, also painted red, so perhaps the colour scheme did take its cue from the name of the house.

The American had returned to his country in the 1950s as he was growing old. He was apparently staying at an old age home somewhere in the Midwest and the bitter winters probably gave him enough time to rue the decision to quit the salubrious environs of Mussoorie. While leaving, he had sold the house to a cheerful Goan widow, Mrs Rebello. Her husband had worked as the manager of Mountain Range Club while she was employed as the housekeeper, and they had lived most of their lives on the premises. When he died, his wife decided to stay on in Mussoorie as their connections with Goa had long gone. Mr Rebello had left his widow in comfortable circumstances, so she decided to buy Redwood Manor when it came on the market.

Mrs Rebello, being accomplished in the art of managing hotels, decided to let out the spare rooms at Redwood Manor for paying guests. The house had five bedrooms and, unusually, five bathrooms as well, having been built on American style of architecture; so it was ideally suited for the purpose. She accordingly placed an advertisement in newspapers distributed across Dehradun and Delhi. Soon enough, the reputation of Redwood Manor as a comfortable abode and its cheerful mistress, who also happened to be an expert cook, spread far and wide, and the good lady found herself with a surfeit of guests to choose from.

Under her smiling, cheerful face, Mrs Rebello hid a sharp mind, honed by dealing with the sometimes-eccentric guests at Mountain Range Club.

Accordingly, she was a little put out when a guest who had made herself known as Miss Anjali Chowdhary arrived at Redwood Manor one summer. From the letter she had received inquiring about a room, she had assumed that the lady would be of a mature age, perhaps a spinster with the means to travel the world. Instead, the person who presented herself at the house was a petite, attractive, young lady around twenty-five years of age. She also seemed a bit unsure of herself as she told Mrs Rebello that she was a writer who had come up to Mussoorie to find some peace and quiet so that she could work on her novel. The whole story seemed a little flimsy, but she fell prey to the appeal, looking at the large, dark eyes that gazed at her apprehensively. Against her better judgement, she allowed the young lady to stay for a week—only after full advance was paid, of course! Sentiment could never be allowed to cloud sound commercial acumen in Mrs Rebello's book.

Anjali Chowdhary had a sunny temperament. She was adept at playing the piano, so the old instrument that the American had left behind was dusted and his old music books unearthed from a storeroom. The piano was hopelessly out of tune but within no time, an old Sardar-ji with a cantankerous expression appeared out of nowhere and proceeded to charm the instrument into a new lease of life.

Mrs Rebello was swept along by Anjali's ebullience and soon the two were singing old songs and cooking great Goan feasts (minus the seafood, of course) in the old-fashioned kitchen. The former contretemps were forgotten and the initial period of a week for Anjali's stay was happily extended. She was from Hisar but as her father was in the army, he had been transferred to various places around the country. The old colonel seemed to be a fearsome character, complete with a walrus moustache and a rasping, parade-ground voice. Anjali's mother had died a few years ago and her father had retired at the same time. They now lived in Chandigarh where her father had built a small house when the new city was being laid out.

It was difficult for Mrs Rebello to establish any familial connection between the gruff army man of Anjali's description with the happy-go-lucky, petite girl in front of her, but perhaps Anjali took after her mother.

Akshay Yadav was the next to arrive. He was a tall young man, rather dark in complexion, with a quiet manner. He said that he had come up to Mussoorie for an interview as a junior executive at Birchwood Hotel. He told Mrs Rebello that he wanted to take a small holiday along with appearing for the interview, which was why he had chosen to stay at Redwood Manor away from the hustle and bustle of the Mall Road where the hotel was located. If Mrs Rebello felt that people who applied for jobs as a junior executive in a hotel were unlikely to be able to afford her not inconsiderable tariff, she hid her scepticism well when handed over a week's advance in cash.

Akshay was not a very communicative person. Dinner that evening brought the small group together. Anjali was at her vivacious best while Akshay ate mostly in silence, though there was a soft smile on his face at Anjali's sallies.

The next few days went by peacefully. Akshay went on long walks every day. He would leave after breakfast and return only by evening. He had requested Mrs Rebello to pack some sandwiches, which would be his picnic lunch. Anjali's routine also changed. She was no longer to be found in Redwood Manor during the day playing the piano or writing. She told Mrs Rebello that she wanted to go down to the Mall Road and window-shop or to visit the bookshops near Lavender Lane. She would leave after Akshay and return before him, so the normally astute Mrs Rebello did not suspect anything.

It was a Saturday morning when the peace of Redwood Manor was rudely shattered. Mrs Rebello was pottering around in the kitchen garden dressed in overalls with an apron and a faded straw hat when the doorbell rang with unaccustomed violence. There was clearly a fierce spirit with his thumb firmly on the bell. Mrs Rebello got up arthritically from a kneeling position near the carrot bed where she was dealing with a recalcitrant outbreak of weeds and stumbled towards the house. She entered from the kitchen and caught a glimpse of her weather-beaten straw hat, which she hastily pulled off, and hurried towards the front door, shedding her apron as she walked.

Meanwhile, the ringing of the doorbell had turned a little hoarse due to unaccustomed overuse. Hearing the asthmatic tone, the person at the door had taken to banging on it loudly such that the door creaked on its hinges. Mrs Rebello walked briskly up to the door and turned the handle. A large figure precipitated itself into the house and fell on top of her. For some time, there was a melee of arms and legs, and a bellowing, red face close to her as they thrashed around on the floor. Then the person slowly stood up. The light of battle shone strongly in Mrs Rebello's eyes as she turned on her assailant.

"Who are you and what do you mean by breaking my door down!" she shouted.

"I did not break your door down, madam! Nobody was answering the bell and then it stopped ringing properly, so I had to bang on the door." The voice who answered her was hoarse and menacing, but she was not deterred.

"Who are you and what is your business?" Mrs Rebello asked in a steely voice.

"I am Colonel Chowdhary," the giant replied loftily.

"So? I don't know anyone of that name," said Mrs Rebello scornfully.

"Do you deny that you are keeping my daughter here under wrongful confinement?" The colonel was now wagging his not inconsiderable forefinger in her face.

"Certainly, I deny it. Nobody is kept under confinement at Redwood Manor," said Mrs Rebello spiritedly, though a light of understanding had dawned in her eyes.

"Do you deny that you have a girl named Anjali Chowdhary staying here?" the colonel bellowed.

"No, why should I deny it? There is a lady by that name staying with us, yes," Mrs Rebello answered calmly.

"So! I knew it! You have kidnapped her, madam, and you will answer for it!" The colonel's salt-and-pepper moustache was blowing in the wind in his agitation.

"I have done nothing of the sort! This is a paying guest establishment, duly licensed by the government," said the worthy lady, gesturing towards the framed certificate on the wall. "She is an adult and staying here of her own free will. And now, I will trouble you to get out of my house or I will call the police!" she concluded on a masterful note.

Two of the menservants of Redwood Manor had entered the hall on hearing the loud voices. They were the chowkidar and the cook, both tall, rangy, Pahadi men, and they formed a protective circle around their mistress. Realising that he was outnumbered, the astute colonel changed tracks. He was a master of tactics, after all!

"I would like to take a room here. Is it available?" The colonel asked in a more controlled voice. Just then the doorbell rang again. This time, it was a more refined ring, or so Mrs Rebello thought based on a lifetime spent in analysing the way that people rang doorbells. Turning away from the irascible colonel, she walked to the door and opened it.

A tall, elegant lady stood at the door. She was dressed in a printed silk sari with a pashmina stole draped around her shoulders. Her immaculately coiffured, short hair had a few streaks of grey that only added to her graceful charm. She carried an expensive handbag and there was an unmistakeable aura of class and sophistication about her. A chauffeur wearing a peaked cap and uniform stood behind her carrying a suitcase.

"Is this Redwood Manor?" she asked in a soft but compelling voice.

"It is, indeed, madam. How can I help you?" Mrs Rebello said.

"I would like to have a room please."

"Most certainly, madam, please come inside," said Mrs Rebello. With that, completely ignoring the long-suffering colonel, the two women walked over to the writing desk that served as the reception counter for Redwood Manor. The colonel watched them go past. There was an appreciative gleam in his eye on seeing the unexpected but undeniably attractive guest who had walked into the house. The formalities were soon completed, and Mrs Rebello escorted the lady to her room with the chauffeur carrying her suitcase. She soon returned to find the colonel pacing up and down the drawing room.

"Well madam, do you have time for other guests who actually came in first?" the colonel said bitingly.

"I have already requested you to leave my house! You leave me with no option but to call the police," said Mrs Rebello.

"I want to take a room in the house on rent," he added in a more placating manner.

Mrs Rebello wavered between avarice and good sense and, as always, the former prevailed. With a sigh, she opened the guest register and proceeded to enter the colonel's name. That done, the colonel was escorted to his room by the chowkidar, and Mrs Rebello heaved a sigh of relief. She sank down on to a sofa and covered her throbbing head with a handkerchief dipped in eau de cologne to calm her shattered nerves. She must have fallen asleep for she woke up with a start to hear the front door opening. Anjali entered the house and, seeing Mrs Rebello lying on the sofa, went up to her and sat down beside her.

Mrs Rebello removed the handkerchief from her face and looked frostily at her.

"You never told me that your father was coming today! He accused me of kidnapping you!" Mrs Rebello sounded agitated.

"Really! He's such a bear!" Anjali said laughingly. She did not seem at all put out by her father's arrival or his antics, but seeing that Mrs Rebello was quite upset, she applied herself to soothing the good lady's nerves.

On Saturday evenings, Mrs Rebello used to host a 'cocktail hour' for her guests. She had barely enough time to change and wash her face before coming down for the event after her untimely sleep. The cook and the serving boys had laid out the drinks tray and had placed freshly cut orange gladioli and tuberoses from the garden into a large cut-glass vase on the coffee table. A plate of canapes, some nuts and wafers had also been placed on the table. The weather was pleasant, so the windows had been left open.

The first guests to walk down the stairs were Anjali and her father. The giant was looking far more presentable in a tweed suit, though Mrs Rebello looked at him askance. Anjali came up and spoke to her placatingly, "I'm really sorry for what happened today morning. The fact is that I had left home without telling my father where I was going," began Anjali. Mrs Rebello opened her mouth to remonstrate as Anjali continued, "We had had an argument. It was one of several, in fact, so I decided to leave in a rage."

"She has always been a firebrand," growled Colonel Chowdhary. The paternal pride in his voice was apparent.

It was evident that he had forgiven his daughter as he had always done in the past. "She wrote to me explaining where she was, so I came here immediately."

"Well, I'm glad you have patched up," said Mrs Rebello dryly. She had not forgiven the colonel for his insinuations. She handed him a glass of whisky and soda which he accepted with alacrity.

Just then Akshay Yadav entered the room, escorting the elegant lady who had arrived that morning. They all turned to look at her and rose to their feet. She was wearing a cream-coloured Banarasi silk sari with a magnificent pearl necklace. Akshay was wearing a dark suit and even had a tie on. Mrs Rebello went forward to greet her guests.

"This is my mother," said Akshay, a shade apologetically.

The revelation was unexpected to say the least. Mrs Rebello gaped. "Your mother?" she chimed in a little foolishly. She was beginning to have visions of flocks of parents and their estranged offspring littered all over her polished parquet floor.

"Yes, I should have told you about her arrival, but I was not sure of the date," said Akshay.

The elegant lady smiled politely at Mrs Rebello and walked up to Anjali. "So, you must be Anjali," she said in her attractive contralto voice.

Anjali blushed but held her ground. "Yes, and this is my father, Colonel Chowdhary. Father, may I introduce Mrs Yadav."

The colonel was looking baffled. "*This* is Mrs Yadav!" The surprise in his voice was so acute that it sounded almost insulting. But he recovered himself quickly. He bowed with old-fashioned grace and took Mrs Yadav's hand in his. She smiled disarmingly at him and the tension in the room palpably lightened.

"I'm sure you were expecting a *junglee*," said Mrs Yadav with a smile.

The colonel spluttered. "No, no, it's just that, you know …" he trailed off incoherently.

"I was expecting an uncouth yahoo myself," said Mrs Yadav, smiling up at him.

Mrs Rebello was feeling out of her depth. It seemed that her disparate guests not only knew each other but had a deep connection that she was unaware of.

"What's all this about?" she asked Anjali as she handed over a glass of wine to Mrs Yadav. "Do all of you know each other?"

"My father doesn't want me to have anything to do with Akshay," began Anjali. "We are Rajputs, you know, while they …" she trailed off, a bit embarrassed by what she was about to say.

"So, you have 'something' to do with Akshay, is it! You never told me. I would have never allowed the two of you to stay under my roof," said Mrs Rebello accusingly.

"That's why we did not tell you," Anjali interrupted with aplomb. She walked up to the suffering landlady and put an arm around her shoulders. "This was the only way that we could get them to meet," she said cajolingly. "Akshay's father passed away when he was a boy, so there is really no one who could come and talk to my father. He can be difficult, as you know."

The 'difficult' colonel was meanwhile regaling Mrs Yadav with tales of hunting and warfare. He was apparently telling her how he had tracked a wounded tiger in the jungles near Nagpur and had killed it with his *khukri*, when his gun jammed. Anjali had heard the stirring tale a few times before, so she was unmoved, but it was evident that Mrs Yadav found the story fascinating. She turned to find Akshay smiling at the two.

"So, now that we are properly chaperoned, I presume you won't have a problem if we take a walk in the moonlight before dinner," said Anjali to Mrs Rebello. "Those two seem quite happy to be with each other."

"Not at all," said Mrs Rebello. "It's a wonderful evening and I need to attend to dinner anyway."

It seemed that their youthful romance may have also sparked off a more mature version in her boarding house that day. Two for the price of one was sure to appeal to Mrs Rebello's parsimonious nature.

11

Oakwoods

The rather nondescript house, with its equally nondescript name, stood on a little patch of land just above Camel's Back Road. It was surrounded by trees, so you could hardly see it from the road. The narrow path leading to the house was also easy to miss. Even the hills it overlooked were not the majestic snow-capped Himalayas but the more modest Vincent Hill with the Convent of Jesus and Mary perched on top. All in all, it was a discreet house, quiet to the point of reticence. The house was painted a light yellow with white window frames and a green roof.

It was apparently owned by a rich seth from Bombay. Mussoorie folk had a habit of attributing ownership of old houses to such seths whether or not there was any truth behind the story. It was a convenient analogy for someone rich, elusive, mysterious, and probably fat. Perhaps the Dev Anand and Raj Kapoor movies, then in vogue, had something to do with this characterisation. Suffice it to say that the elusive seth never came up to Mussoorie. He had authorised Bajaj and Co., the estate agents, to rent out the house every season. This was an easy task as the house was rented by the same person year after year for the months of May and June. Every year, sometime in April, a letter would arrive requesting for the booking.

> M/S Bajaj and Co., Estate Agents,
> Near Rialto Cinema,
> The Mall,
> Mussoorie
> 12 April 1962
> Dear Sirs,
> I wish to take Oakwoods on rent for May and June 1962. I am enclosing my cheque drawn on the First Bank of India, Mussoorie, for the full amount of the rent. Please leave the keys in the letterbox as usual to await my arrival on 1 May.
> Yours sincerely,
> Avinash Gupta
> 103, South Side Colony
> New Delhi

Bajaj and Co. had a well-oiled routine once the letter enclosing the cheque from Mr Gupta was received. They knew the reclusive habits of their client, hence there would be no one to receive him when he arrived. The front door key was kept in the letterbox near the wicket gate close to the house so that he could let himself in. The estate agents sent a cleaning woman to the house the day before his arrival. Mr Gupta had no contact with the company. Perhaps, he had met them when he had started this arrangement three years ago, but there was no one at Bajaj who remembered what he looked like.

It was on 17 August that a police inspector from Delhi, accompanied by his local counterpart, called at the Bajaj office in Mussoorie inquiring about Mr Gupta. Apparently, he had not come home at the end of June, and after waiting for some time, his wife had approached the police in Delhi.

Mrs Gupta had driven up to the police station in South Side Colony. It was a blazing hot and damp day in July. She had met the station house officer (SHO) there.

"My husband is missing," said Mrs Gupta in Hindi.

"I see. When did you see him last and what is your name?" the SHO started with the series of questions. Mrs Gupta appeared calm, but there was an underlying tension about her.

"My name is Aparna Gupta, and I last saw him at the end of April."

"So long ago! Why have you taken so much time to report the matter?" the SHO asked.

"My husband is a trader in yarn and cloth. He usually travels to South India to meet the suppliers in May and June. During this period, it is very hard to contact him as he visits small towns and he's too busy to write. He always comes back by the end of June. This year, he went away as usual, but when he did not come back by end of June, I came to register a complaint," said Mrs Gupta.

The SHO took down all the particulars and prepared a statement for Mrs Gupta to sign. He also asked her for her husband's photograph and his office address. He told her that the police would investigate and revert with any progress after a week.

The police visited Mr Gupta's office in Old Delhi the very next day. His munshi met them and expressed complete ignorance about his master's whereabouts. He acknowledged that Mr Gupta was usually away in May and June, but he was unaware of where he went. His responsibilities were restricted to managing the office and he did not know anything about the commercial side of things. The other employees were too junior to know anything.

A lead finally came from the railway authorities. The inspector assigned to the case had asked the railways to check for all reservations made on 30 April, the day that Mrs Gupta had last seen her husband. The railways reported that there actually was a reservation for Mr and Mrs Avinash Gupta for Dehradun in an air-conditioned coupe of the Mussoorie Express that left on the night of 30 April from Old Delhi Railway Station. Railway records confirmed that the couple had indeed travelled on the train as their tickets had been checked by a travelling ticket examiner (TTE) after the train had left Delhi.

Armed with this information, the police visited Mrs Gupta at her house in South Side Colony. It was evident that the Guptas were well-off. The police inspector confronted

Mrs Gupta with the information they had obtained from the railways.

"I did not travel to Dehradun on 30 April, Inspector Saheb," said Mrs Gupta confidently.

"But there was a reservation in your name, madam, and the TTE had checked your tickets."

"I am telling you that I did not travel to Dehradun. There must be some mistake," Mrs Gupta retorted emphatically. "In fact, I have never been to Dehradun or Mussoorie at all."

The inspector was not able to find a chink in her statement. He went back to Old Delhi Railway Station and, acting on a hunch, asked for the reservation records of the Mussoorie Express for previous years. These were made available after a wait as soon as the records were obtained from a storeroom. He went through them and there it was! As regular as clockwork for the last three years—there was a booking for Mr and Mrs Avinash Gupta from Delhi to Dehradun on 30 April. It was evident that if Mrs Gupta had not travelled to Dehradun, it had to be someone who was passing herself off as her.

This train of thought led the police to the obvious conclusion that there was a second woman involved in the case. They went back to question Mrs Gupta, but they were unable to get further information from her. The police now shifted their focus on Mr Gupta's friends to try and find out whether any one of them knew about his involvement with another woman. One of his college friends told the police that Avinash Gupta had been involved with a woman named Madhuri Prasad when they were in college.

Madhuri's parents being orthodox and conservative had objected to the relationship, as Avinash was not from their caste. They took their daughter away from college and got her married to someone from their own caste. That was the last that Avinash's friends had heard of Madhuri. Her family was from Aligarh, so presumably, she had gone back there. The police decided to follow up the lead. The Prasad family in Aligarh that Madhuri belonged to was fairly well known as her father was a senior officer in the state government. Mr Prasad received the police inspector at his home and told him his daughter's story.

"Yes, Inspector Saheb. It is true that Madhuri had got involved with a boy from a different caste in Delhi. It was absolutely unacceptable to us, so I brought her back with me to Aligarh. Here, she got married to Ajay Chandra who was an accountant." The old man paused to regain his balance and then continued, "Ajay turned out to be a drunk. He beat my daughter mercilessly." The old man was trembling as he relived the horror that his daughter had undergone. "At last, I agreed that they should go separate ways, and they got divorced four years ago."

The inspector nodded. "What happened after that?"

"It was impossible for Madhuri to remain in Aligarh. People were already whispering about her and my position in the government was becoming difficult," said Mr Prasad with his head bowed. It was obvious that he was ashamed of what he had done to his daughter.

"So, what happened?" The inspector asked.

"Madhuri got a job as a schoolteacher in Ghaziabad. She had completed her graduation after she came back from Delhi, and I knew someone who could help her out. She lives in Ghaziabad now," said Mr Prasad.

"Is she in touch with you?"

"I am too ashamed to talk to her. She is in touch with her mother," Mr Prasad replied, with his head bowed.

"May we speak to your wife?" the inspector questioned. Mr Prasad nodded and called out for his wife to join them. She soon did. Mrs Prasad was a plump lady with a *ghoonghat* covering her head. The inspector asked her about her daughter. She replied with what composure could be expected in the circumstances. Yes, her daughter was living in Ghaziabad. They wrote occasionally to each other and had met once when she had travelled to be with her. She seemed happy.

Mrs Prasad went inside and brought out a bunch of letters stored in a biscuit jar. The latest was dated 10 April and talked of mundane things. The inspector thanked the Prasads and noted their daughter's Ghaziabad address before parting.

He visited Ghaziabad after returning from Aligarh. He went to the address given by Mrs Prasad only to find the house locked. The neighbours were quite happy to talk to the police. Yes, Madhuri Prasad (she had reverted to her maiden name after her divorce) did indeed live there. She was a friendly person who also gave tuitions to the neighbouring children. She had gone away for the summer holidays as she always did but this time had not returned when school began in July. The neighbours were just beginning to worry when the inspector arrived. They had met Madhuri's mother when she had visited, and they had assumed that Madhuri would be going to her parents' place for the summer vacation. The inspector did not correct this assumption.

The house lock was broken by the police. Inside, everything was kept neatly in its right place but covered with a thin film of dust. On the table by the bed was a framed photograph of Madhuri and Avinash Gupta. It appeared to be a recent photo and was taken in front of a house with hills in the background. The case seemed to be progressing quite rapidly now. Clearly, the mystery woman who had travelled with Avinash Gupta was Madhuri, and they seemed to have been holidaying in Mussoorie.

The inspector immediately sent word to the police station in Kulri, Mussoorie, and decided to go there himself. He reached Mussoorie on 16 August.

The SHO at Kulri Police Station offered tea to his colleague from Delhi while he briefed him on the case. After almost an hour, the inspector handed over the framed photograph to his colleague, who studied it carefully.

"This certainly seems like a house in the hills, but I can't immediately confirm whether it is in Mussoorie," the SHO said at last.

"How can we identify it?" the inspector asked.

"If it is a rented house, it would have come through one of the estate agents. There are not too many of them. We can start visiting them tomorrow," said the SHO as it had already become dark. The inspector thanked him and agreed to meet at ten the next morning.

The Bajaj office was the first place that the two policemen visited the next morning. Ravi Bajaj hurried over to meet them.

"How can I help you, sir?" Ravi asked.

"Can you identify the people in this photograph and the house?" the inspector inquired.

Ravi took the photo and looked at it carefully. "The man looks familiar and so does the house, but I can't be sure." He called over an employee and introduced him. "Mr Agrawal looks after the rented properties."

Mr Agrawal said immediately, "That is Oakwoods."

"Do you recognise the people in the photo?" the inspector asked.

"Let me explain, inspector. It's rather an odd situation," said Ravi. He proceeded to brief the policemen about the reclusive Mr Gupta and why the estate agents were unable to identify him. After a fairly long narrative during which he was admonished by the SHO about the lax procedures followed by the estate agency, the whole story was finally clear.

"We would like to visit the house," said the SHO. Ravi and Mr Agrawal joined the policemen in their jeep and drove down the Mall Road towards Mussoorie Library.

They turned right on to Camel's Back Road and stopped soon afterwards at the base of the path leading to Oakwoods. They walked up and Mr Agrawal opened the front door. Inside, the house looked very clean and tidy.

"We had the house cleaned after Mr Gupta left at the end of June," said Mr Agrawal. Meanwhile, the two policemen were walking through the house. In the bedroom, on the bedside table, there was a copy of the photograph that they had picked up from Ghaziabad. Clearly, this was the house where the two had been discreetly spending time over the years. The rest of the house yielded no clues, hence, after a thorough search, the policemen walked out into the sunlight.

"I wonder what happened after they came to Mussoorie," mused the SHO.

"Well, one thing is that they should have booked their tickets for going back," said the inspector.

"We should go to the railway booking office and find out," said the SHO. The railways did not come up to Mussoorie as the nearest railhead was Dehradun. However, they maintained what was known in railway parlance as an 'out agency' in Mussoorie. This was located near Head Post Office on the slope leading down to the jhulaghar. The police jeep covered the distance in a short while and soon the policemen were in discussion with the manager of the out agency.

The first thing he could confirm was that there was no booking made for Mr and Mrs Gupta from Dehradun to Delhi at the end of June. They looked at all the dates around that period, but nothing could be found. As a precaution, they checked bookings made for other trains leaving Dehradun to any destination, but there were none. The policemen then demanded for records from previous years. Sure enough, for the past three years, Mr and Mrs Gupta had been booking an air-conditioned coupe on the Mussoorie Express on 30 June from Dehradun to Delhi. The policemen thanked the manager and left with the booking files as potential evidence.

"It is as clear as day," said the SHO. "The couple came up to Mussoorie as they have been doing for the past three years, but they did not leave by train this year. I wonder where they went, and why."

"I think the 'why' part is obvious. There does not seem to be any evidence of foul play. I mean, no bodies have been found or anything of the sort. I think they just wanted to disappear together," said the inspector.

The SHO nodded. "That sounds like the most likely explanation."

The inspector took his leave after having a cup of tea at Kulri Police Station. He was anxious to get back to Delhi and file his report.

He met the superintendent of police (SP) in Delhi the next day and told him what he had found.

"Sir, it is evident that Madhuri Prasad and Avinash Gupta were having an affair. From whatever we can make out, his wife was unaware of the situation; hence she does not seem to have a motive to do away with them. They had been very discreet about it and the holidays in Mussoorie were cleverly planned for some time. I cannot speculate on what was their motive behind running away together, but that is what they seem to have done. We can try to look for them, but it is also true that they have committed no crime and indeed, no crime has been committed at all. In my opinion, the case should be closed," said the inspector.

"You have a point," added the SP musingly. "Perhaps the pressure of living a double life was too much. What are you going to tell Mrs Gupta?"

"We will have to tell her what we believe happened. It will be a difficult discussion, but it can't be helped. I will not go into detail with Mr Prasad. Just tell him that we are unable to trace his daughter. He will probably feel that the police is incompetent, but that is what a lot of people feel anyway," said the inspector a shade cynically.

The SP agreed to this course of action and the case was closed with a noting that Avinash Gupta and Madhuri Prasad had gone missing of their own accord.

The inspector called on Mr Prasad first. By now, the family had got accustomed to thinking that their daughter may not come back. The inspector stopped short of telling the family about the suspected affair but did say that it appeared that she had left of her own accord and that no foul play was suspected. Mr Prasad and his wife were saddened by the news, but eventually accepted that their daughter may have wanted a more vibrant life of her own. The inspector left them hoping that she would be in touch with them soon.

The meeting with Mrs Gupta was more complex. She opened the door for the inspector herself as it appeared that there was no one else in the house. They sat down in the drawing room with the inspector taking a straight-backed chair across from where she was sitting on a sofa. Her expression was neutral, though her eyes were a little wary. The inspector did not notice that Mrs Gupta's face was masked by a shadow.

"Mrs Gupta, we have made some progress in the case, and I wanted to inform you about what we have found," began the inspector. He spoke a little awkwardly and his tone was rigidly formal.

"I see. Please continue," said Mrs Gupta in an even voice.

"It seems that your husband was having an affair," said the inspector. He paused as Mrs Gupta turned her head away.

She had read the note in her husband's coat pocket almost two years ago. It was a short note, full of love and longing, and it had turned her stomach. Later, she had followed him as he drove to Ghaziabad that night. He had made a pretext of a sudden business meeting, but he had never left the house at such short notice before. She had hailed an autorickshaw and followed his car, which eventually stopped in front of a house where a woman stood waiting for him. He had gone in and after a long interval, she had looked in through an open window on the ground floor. It was enough. She had stumbled out of the house and blindly taken an autorickshaw back home.

The inspector spoke again after she had regained her composure somewhat, though her eyes were full of tears.

"I'm sorry, Mrs Gupta. I could not break the news in any other way," said the inspector apologetically. "The woman is someone he knew from his college days. Her name is Madhuri Prasad."

She had met many of his old friends and some of them had become her friends too. On a convivial evening, they had started telling stories about their days in college and past affairs and crushes. Madhuri's name had come up and it had confirmed what Mrs Gupta had read on the nameplate of the house in Ghaziabad.

"They used to go to Mussoorie together every summer. They had been going there for the past three years," the inspector added.

Mrs Gupta did not say anything but listened quietly with her head bowed.

Mrs Gupta had boarded the train and latched the door of the coupe from inside. She made a bed for her 'husband' on the upper berth using some pillows and covered them with a blanket to give the impression of someone sleeping. She then lay down on the lower berth and waited for the train to start. Soon afterwards, the train crossed the Iron Bridge over the Yamuna when there was a knock at the door. She got up and opened the door to see the TTE standing there.

"Tickets please, madam."

She turned back and took out the tickets from her handbag. The TTE glanced at them and the sleeping 'man' on the top berth and ticked off the passengers. Mr and Mrs Gupta had been duly accounted for.

"This year, they went to Mussoorie as usual. They stayed in a house called Oakwoods, which is where they had been staying every year. However, they did not book a return ticket to Delhi or to any other place. They have just disappeared," said the inspector.

Mrs Gupta gasped. She got up and poured two glasses of water. She handed one over to the inspector who drank it thirstily. He was sweating in the warm room. She turned away from him and drank some water herself.

The horror of the last day was fresh in her memory. The sudden violence and the emotions, long suppressed, finding an outlet. Later, after she returned from Mussoorie, she drove to the remote jungle road near Bharatpur which she had scouted the previous year. There she disposed of the bodies. There were many wild animals around and, with luck, the bodies would never be found.

"I see, inspector. Do you think they have disappeared of their own accord?" Mrs Gupta said in a composed voice.

"That is what it looks like, madam."

"So, the case is closed?" Mrs Gupta asked.

"Yes, the case is closed," said the inspector as he rose to take his leave.

12

Pine Hayes

Suraj Bhan, Akash Malhotra, and Jagjit Singh were childhood friends. They had gone to school together and each more reluctantly than the other had somehow managed to graduate with barely passing marks from a nondescript college in West Delhi. Soon afterwards, all three were installed on the gaddis of their family businesses in the wholesale markets of Delhi. Suraj Bhan was steeped in spices in Khari Baoli, while his friends were pitchforked into the hosiery and footwear trade. Time passed and the three friends pursued a predictable path: marriage, children, and an increasing waistline with a commensurate decline in the volume of hair on their heads.

A faint spicy odour followed Suraj around wherever he went, and the others joked that they needed only to cut the potatoes and onions and wave the plate around him to get pakoras. Akash's shoes were a dead giveaway of his trade. Shiny and pointy, made of patent leather, they gave him a rolling gait. With his slightly bowed legs, he sometimes gave the impression of being a seaman if it was not for his rather prominent paunch. Jagjit was the tallest. He wore glasses and read newspapers in English and was thus considered the most intellectual of the trio.

"Yaar, our life is passing us by," said Jagjit reflectively. It was a balmy evening in March and the three friends were comfortably ensconced on the terrace of Suraj's house. It was their traditional get-together on the last Saturday of the month. A bottle of Black Castle whisky had been broached, chicken tikkas, pakoras, aloo tikkis, and all manner of snacks had been provided by the womenfolk who were engrossed in their own comfortable gossip in the drawing room below.

"Oye, what has happened to you?" Akash asked, turning to Jagjit. "Are you okay?"

"What have we done in life? All we did was what our fathers did before us and our sons will do afterwards," Jagjit added, his voice trailing off.

"So, what's wrong with that?" Suraj jumped in.

"Nothing, yaar. Only..." Jagjit remained contemplative.

"This is true. We haven't really done anything exciting in life," said Akash. "Wake up, take a bath if there is water, have parathas, start the scooter, drive to the shop and sit on the gaddi the whole day. The people we meet are also the same day after day."

Suraj contributed to it, "Have samosas, chole bhature and jalebi for lunch. Come home after the kids have gone to sleep, listen to the wife complaining. Get shouted at if you have a drink. Have dinner and go to sleep."

Suraj refilled their glasses. It was a double Patiala this time, they drank in silence for a while. The strains of a Shammi Kapoor dance number filtered through from downstairs.

By this time, the whisky had started to kick in.

"Yaar, let us go to Mussoorie." Akash was the first to break the reverie.

The others turned to look at him in some astonishment. He had obviously been carried away by visions of Shammi Kapoor cavorting in a Mussoorie hotel with an admiring Asha Parekh and a glamorous chorus line.

"It will be a change," added Akash. "My brother-in-law had gone there last year, and he had a great time."

"With family?" Suraj asked.

"No! Only three of us!" Akash declared excitedly.

The three friends digested this revolutionary thought in silence. Almost instinctively, Suraj refilled their glasses from the rapidly depleting bottle, and they drank in silence. Dutch courage was required, as they still had to break the news to their sceptical and disapproving spouses who were already calling them for dinner. They stumbled down the stairs and sat down at the dinner table, avoiding their wives' eyes.

Finally, when the gulab jamuns arrived, Akash could not hold it in any longer.

"We are going to Mussoorie," he whispered, avoiding looking directly at anyone. Since his mouth was full of the luscious sweet, nobody understood him.

"What did you say, ji?" Akash's wife said.

"We are going to Mussoorie!" Jagjit announced.

"Who's going to Mussoorie?" Jagjit's wife asked.

"We three are going to Mussoorie," Suraj clarified, gesturing towards his friends.

There was pandemonium at the dinner table at this blatant, and unexpected, act of rebellion. It was only after suitable peace overtures had been made and accepted that the ladies allowed their menfolk to slip their leash.

As it happens, the women had been discussing the fabulous new salwar suits that had come on sale at their friend Pammi's shop in Sadar Bazaar and they had been wondering how to convince the menfolk to allow them to buy. The Mussoorie trip was a heaven-sent opportunity to apply a quid pro quo so they all arose from the dining table giddy with excitement for their shopping plans and trips to Mussoorie.

"Where will we stay in Mussoorie?" Jagjit raised the next obvious question. "Hotels are too expensive."

"My brother-in-law stayed at a guest house. It's called Pine Hayes," said Akash. He told them what he had learnt, and the others agreed that it was a good option. Accordingly, they sent off a telegram to the property and soon a reply arrived, confirming their booking for a week in May. They also booked second-class tickets on the Mussoorie Express and now the whole trip began to appear more real.

"I think we should buy coats. It's cold there," suggested Jagjit. They all had coats already as it was cold in winter in Delhi too, but the tacit agreement was that their battered old coats would not suffice for the stylish summer crowd of Mussoorie. Accordingly, tweed coats of rather startling hues were procured and carefully stowed away in suitcases, packing for the trip having started almost two weeks before they were leaving.

Not being accustomed to travelling, even the simple act of catching a train from Delhi station took on an air of excitement. They did not sleep much and arrived at Dehradun station a little bleary-eyed. They got into a bus to Mussoorie that stopped with a jerk every few minutes to pick up passengers and rivalled a racing car in between. Conversation soon dried up and the three friends were looking distinctly green at the gills by the time the bus reached the halfway house. When the bus finally stopped at the Mussoorie Library bus stand, they emerged wondering if the trip was really worth it at all. They haggled with the coolies half-heartedly, with none of the elan that they displayed in business. Soon they were walking on the road towards Wild Rose Hotel. Pine Hayes was located just above the road as it wound its way along.

The guest house was a distinctly ramshackle establishment, clearly catering to a lower-middle-class clientele. The name Pine Hayes was derived from a row of rather decrepit pine trees that formed a border at the back of the building. The squarish, double-storeyed building topped by a rusting tin roof had been divided into 'suites' which comprised a bedroom, a small kitchenette, and a bathroom. The partitions were all made of wood, so you could hear everything that your neighbours said or did. Entering the building, one came across a central courtyard covered by a tin roof. There was a small reception desk where the proprietor sat. This worthy was a gruff man from eastern Uttar Pradesh who insisted on advance payment for the whole week before letting them in. The suites had a balcony, but it was covered with a wire mesh, presumably to prevent errant tenants from escaping without paying their bills.

In order to save money, they had taken only one suite and had asked for an extra cot to be put in. After that had been installed, there was virtually no place to move around. Their suite was on the first floor at the back, so they had to carry their heavy suitcases across the courtyard and then up the stairs. The three fell into an exhausted sleep after reaching their room only to wake up as the sun was going down. There was no catering in Pine Hayes, so they got dressed and walked down to the Library. The Mall Road was crowded, full of summer visitors. Hand-pulled rickshaws with stylishly attired women went past them as did a few gentlemen on horses. The pedestrians, like them, were mostly middle-class folk and workers. They trudged along, still groggy after the tiring journey.

"Let's stop and have something to eat," said Akash. They were standing in front of The Glass Room, a restaurant that had a live band and a bar. There was light streaming out of the windows on the first floor. "Shall we go in here?"

The others hesitated. They had undoubtedly been to a few restaurants in Delhi but none of them looked as fancy as this one. The men were all wearing ties and jackets and the women were dressed in silk sarees.

"Let's not go today," said Jagjit finally, voicing their collective apprehension. "It's very crowded and we may not find a place to sit."

"There's a *halwai* nearby. Let's go there," said Suraj, pointing towards an establishment that had jalebis frying outside in a large *karahi*. The others acquiesced and they all walked into Rastogi Sweets to have dinner.

Later, as they walked back to Pine Hayes, the conversation was all about the dinner. Clearly, Mr Rastogi could not hope to rival the quality and taste that their wives could produce! It started drizzling as they walked, and they were quite wet by the time they got to their dingy room. Too tired for anything, they just changed and slept.

There was bright sunshine the next day. Cheered by this, the three went out and had parathas at Rastogi Sweets for breakfast—it was a bit difficult to break the habit of a lifetime. They wandered around the Mall Road in their bright tweed coats, sweating as the warmer weather made the coats a bit redundant. After some desultory window-shopping at Kulri, they had lunch at a clone of Rastogi Sweets, went back to Pine Hayes, and slept. So far, their holiday was turning out to be quite sedate and rather unlike the Shammi Kapoor fantasies that they had been nursing.

In the evening, buoyed by their rest, they bought half a bottle of Black Castle whisky, along with some namkeen from near the Library, and went off into a quiet road leading down from the Mall Road. Feeling very adventurous, they drank the whisky in the open while keeping a sharp eye for patrolling policemen.

"Yaar, we definitely have to do something today," said Akash as the whisky warmed their insides.

"What?" Jagjit said.

"Did you notice the fancy hotel that we passed by in the morning?" Akash said.

"Which one?" Suraj asked.

"I think it's called White Palisades," said Akash. "It's quite near."

"So?" Suraj asked, though he knew what was coming.

"Let's go there for dinner," Akash concluded.

There was a long silence. Then, with one accord, they got up, threw the debris of their namkeens and the whisky bottle by the side of the bench they were sitting on and started walking towards White Palisades Hotel.

The hotel was right on the Mall Road. It was accessed through a large door up a small flight of steps leading to a passage opening out into the reception. Beyond that was the restaurant. There was a live band, and a bar attached to the restaurant. The door was guarded by a fierce doorman from Rajasthan. Tall and broad with large, upturned moustaches and a maroon-and-grey uniform with a tall turban, he was an imposing sight.

The three friends arrived at the door and tried to push it open. The doorman stopped them from doing that and asked in a tough voice as to what they wanted. Jagjit replied as he was the tallest, but still a good ten inches shorter than the doorman, that they wanted to have dinner at the hotel. Rather reluctantly, the doorman opened the door and let them in.

They stopped at the top of a few stairs that led down to the reception. Suraj stumbled and fell down with a thud. He was not hurt but winded. A hotel staff member came running up, with the manager at his heels. Suraj had meantime been helped up by his friends.

The manager had taken in the enormity of the tweed coats. He spoke in a brusque voice in English, "What can I do for you? This is a private hotel."

Jagjit replied in a small voice, "We want to have dinner here."

"I see," said the manager. His eyebrows had gone up a trifle. "We are full at the moment. Do you have a reservation?"

"No," said Jagjit.

The manager continued, "I'm afraid we have a dress code. You need a tie and jacket for dining here."

The three friends were looking quite bewildered by now. For some reason, the manager took pity on them and said, "Follow me. I will see what can be done."

Suitably chastened, the three followed the manager into the restaurant. It was fairly empty, but he led them to a poky little table right next to a trolley full of cutlery and linen.

The three sat down and took in their surroundings. There was a band playing a catchy number that they did not recognise—the theme song from 'Come September'. A few couples were dancing, the women dressed either in frocks or expensive saris and the men in dark suits with thin ties. They looked down ruefully at their tweed coats, but nothing could be done now! At the table, there was a small triangular board that read "Cover Charge Rs 50".

"What is this cover charge?" Suraj said in a stage whisper, but his friends could not enlighten him. Just then a waiter came up and handed them a menu card apiece. He then left without any conversation, leaving them to leaf through it.

"A cup of tea is Rs 2! This is very expensive," said Akash worriedly.

They looked through the menu and finally settled on the bare minimum that they could order to assuage their hunger. A waiter came up to take their order.

"That's all you want?" The waiter asked in Hindi, a touch superciliously.

"Yes," Jagjit responded, glaring at him. He was feeling oppressed by the attitude of the people around him. The waiter backed away and soon their food arrived.

They ate in silence. The food was not great, and it was soon over. The waiter came up and they asked for the bill. It arrived shortly, totalling Rs 150! There was also no break-up of the dishes they had ordered, which would not have added up to even Rs 100. The waiter was summoned again.

"What is this Rs 150?" Jagjit asked. "We did not order so much."

"There is a cover charge here," said the waiter, gesturing towards the triangular notice kept on their table.

"What is this cover charge?" Jagjit couldn't help asking.

"It's the minimum you have to pay per head for sitting in this restaurant," answered the waiter, impatiently. He had other tables to attend to and he did not want to spend any more time with them.

"What! That means we can order more?" Akash asked.

"Not now. This bill has already been cut. If you order any more, it will be another Rs 150," the waiter explained.

There was no escape. They paid the bill and stumbled out of the restaurant. The restaurant was now filled to capacity and the crowd was jitterbugging to the tune of 'Jailhouse Rock' as they fled the place.

The night air was cool, steadying their nerves.

"Yaar, we have made asses of ourselves," said Jagjit.

"I'm still hungry," said Akash plaintively. They were passing by Rastogi Sweets, so they plunged in and had a hearty dinner. It was fairly late by the time they finished. It was past eleven o'clock by the time they started walking back to Pine Hayes.

The road was unusually crowded at this time of the night with some people walking about and some running. They had reached Riviera Hotel when they heard the cry of "Fire!" The crowd of bystanders had grown and as they asked people what had happened, somebody told them that a fire had broken out at Pine Hayes. They started running towards the guest house and soon reached the top of the slope to see the building engulfed in flames. There were a few policemen trying to hold the crowd back and some people, holding buckets, had formed a chain and were trying to douse the flames by throwing water at the building.

"All our things are inside!" Akash cried out.

"We have to take them out!" Suraj yelled.

The thought of losing their possessions moved them to run towards the building, not paying any heed to the potential danger. They struggled to brush aside the feeble attempts of the policemen to hold them back.

They ran into the courtyard and looked around them. Flames were licking the dry wooden walls, and it was only a matter of time before the building would go up completely in flames. Just then, they heard a child crying. A little girl was wandering around alone. Without thinking, Suraj picked her up and ran to the gate. The others just stood where they were for a while and then started running towards the stairs leading to their suite, but it was already engulfed in fire. Just then the perpendicular wing went up with a woosh. The two friends were stumbling back to the courtyard when they heard cries from one of the suites close to where they were standing.

They saw that the door was bolted from the inside. They banged on the door but nobody opened it. Finally, Jagjit kicked the door, and the flimsy wood gave way almost immediately. Inside they found an old couple who were cowering on the bed. Hurriedly, the two friends covered the couple with blankets and helped them out from the room. The fire had intensified, but fortunately they were able to reach the gate.

The crowds outside had swelled considerably. The fire brigade had also arrived and were rigging up their water hoses. However, by then, the wooden structure was well and truly ablaze, and it would burn itself out fairly soon.

A younger woman came rushing to them and embraced the old couple. She was crying copiously and fell at the feet of the two friends, thanking them for saving her parents. They were soon joined by Suraj who had handed over the little girl to her family. A huge crowd collected around the three friends, thanking them and calling them heroes. Soon a man appeared with a camera and said that he was from the press. They had their picture taken and the man was interviewing them when a police inspector came up. He shook hands with the three and thanked them profusely for their bravery. Thanks to them, no lives had been lost in the fire. They were truly heroes!

The rest of the night passed in a whirl. A man came up and said that he was the owner of a nearby hotel and that he would be honoured to give them a free room to stay in. The crowd cheered and after many handshakes and backslapping, the three friends accompanied him to his hotel. It was early morning by then and streaks of dawn were lighting up the sky. The luxurious beds in the hotel were heaven-sent and they fell asleep only to wake up at lunchtime. The local MLA had come to see them and there were more photographs and handshakes all around.

That evening, they left for Dehradun and caught the night train to Delhi. From the station, they engaged a three-wheeler to take them home. As they drove into their colony's narrow streets, people saw them and started running behind the autorickshaw. When they stopped at Suraj Bhan's house that came first on their way, a small crowd gathered. Somebody was waving the *Dainik Milap* clipping that carried their photos and stories prominently. The entire mohalla had seen the stories and as word spread, people came out of their houses with garlands. A small band even put up a performance in their honour! Their families welcomed them with tika and aarti, and everyone wanted to hear the whole story from the horse's mouth.

The heroes had returned home victorious.

13

Oliver's Castle

His Highness Shatrujeet Singh of Kanhapur was almost a caricature of the 'tall, dark and handsome' prince, the beloved of romance novelists. He was fair by perceived Indian standards, but we are talking of a European sensibility here. Tiring of the tiger hunts and the damp solitude of his ancestral seat in the Terai region, he would often come up to Mussoorie with whichever bird of paradise was holding his attention for the moment. When asked why he chose Mussoorie instead of Nainital for his mountain retreat, especially as the latter was so close to his estate, he shrugged his broad shoulders and said in an attractive drawl obviously acquired during his sojourn at Oxford:

"Nainital is just so provincial, old boy," thus nonchalantly disposing of the rival claims of the hill station by the lake.

Shatrujeet's (Shatru to his friends) arrival in Mussoorie was always a spectacle. His black 1947 Buick 8 somehow managed to navigate the crowded Landour bazaar and, even more surprisingly, ascend the steep slope up to Char Dukan, the eponymous little market near St Paul's Church at the start of the circular walk around the summit of Lal Tibba. After that, the road to Oliver's Castle was a comfortable saunter with spectacular snow views as you came on to the northern side. The Buick was driven by his trusted chauffeur, Ram Singh, and he was invariably accompanied by his current inamorata who was usually dressed inappropriately against the cold and used the weather as a convenient excuse to snuggle closer to His redoubtable Highness.

Oliver's Castle was indeed a royal home. Commanding one of the best views in Mussoorie, it was set on a promontory jutting out from Lal Tibba with a panoramic view of the snow-capped mountains. There was no other house within sight and the imposing mansion that the Buick drove up to looked regal yet inviting as the rays of the setting sun glinted on the rooftops. Shatru's father had purchased the house from a departing Englishman and had expanded and improved the accommodation to meet his exacting requirements.

Thankfully, His late, lamented Highness was no longer around to see the shenanigans being enacted by his only son and heir. Shatru and his inamorata were welcomed by his butler with the whole staff in attendance. They sat down for tea on the circular veranda that overlooked the Himalayas.

"What do we *do* in Mussoorie?" Joyce asked, for such was the name of the current royal fancy. Her accent had an Anglo-Indian lilt, and her curly hair had a tinge of brown muddying the black. Her uptilted snub nose and milky complexion were enough to hold Shatru's straying attention at least for the nonce. She was dressed in a calf-length dress with a plunging neckline that she used to good effect to bring her wavering cavalier to heel whenever she felt him straying.

"Oh, this and that," said Shatru.

"What does that mean?" Joyce got up and with her hands on her hips was looking down at Shatru who was lounging on an outdoor sofa.

"You know. A bit of riding and socialising and then there's the Garden Party," added Shatru, his tone emphasising the last two words.

"Ah that! It should be exciting." Joyce sounded enthusiastic.

"Now there's a good girl!" Shatru exclaimed, affectionately patting her on the behind. "Run along, will you, darling; I have some work to discuss with my manager." Thus adjured, Joyce took herself off and left Shatru to his own devices.

The annual garden party at Oliver's Castle was quite definitely *the* social event of the peak tourist season in Mussoorie. Everyone who was anyone was seen in their best and brightest at the gathering. The food was spectacular and the wine world-class. Socialites and businessmen, film stars and musicians, politicians and royalty rubbed shoulders on the elegant lawns of Oliver's Castle, the spectacular backdrop of the Himalayas adding to the milieu. The house was full of guests who stayed for a week and many others came up from Delhi, Bombay, and Calcutta only for the party.

Proceedings began in the early evening just before sunset when the snows were aflame with red and orange and went on under the light of the full moon, for the party was invariably timed to coincide with Vesak, the nirvana day for the Buddha, in May. At night, as the snows glowed with a cold, silvery, ethereal light, a faint chill descended, and the music played on till dawn broke over the Himalayan peaks.

"Ah Robert. How are you?" Shatru asked his Anglo-Indian manager who approached discreetly.

"Very well indeed, Your Highness. I trust the journey was not very tiring," said Robert. He spoke in a low voice. Dressed in a black suit with a tie, he looked like a butler of the old school. He was an invaluable member of Shatru's staff, one who knew everything about the household and His Highness's affairs and one who could be trusted to manage things to perfection. Based in Kanhapur, Robert travelled up to Mussoorie in advance to ensure that Oliver's Castle was in perfect condition for His Highness's visit.

"How are the preparations for the Garden Party coming along?" Shatru asked, coming straight down to business.

"The invitations have been sent out as per our old guest list. If you need to add some people, let me know," Robert added.

Shatru nodded and took out a folded piece of paper and handed it to Robert, saying, "These are the additional people to be invited."

"We have been able to get hold of Rock Henry to perform for the party," informed Robert.

"My word! That's rather grand!" Shatru was impressed. "Is he coming all the way from England just for the party?"

"Well, not really. Apparently, he wanted to come to visit Lucknow, where he was born, and the dates were convenient," said Robert.

"Has the maharani confirmed that she is coming?" Shatru asked.

Robert knew exactly who his master was referring to. "Yes, Your Highness, the Maharani of Sartajpur has confirmed that she will be coming. Apparently, the Maharaja will be coming too. I have allotted the Garden Suite to them," said Robert.

"What! That old coot!" Shatru exclaimed and then said more reflectively, "That queers the pitch somewhat."

The rest of the conversation focused on the people who would be coming to stay at Oliver's Castle, the menus, the allocation of the rooms, and many other details. Shatru displayed a keen attention to detail, quite unlike the languid beau that Joyce thought him to be. There were still ten days left for the Garden Party and their house guests would start arriving in a few days from now. Though there was a lot to be done, under Robert's masterful stewardship, everything moved smoothly.

Shatru and Joyce spent their days riding horses, which she hated, and promenading on the Mall Road, which she loved. The month of May had seen an onrush of summer visitors and Shatru was greeted by many of his friends and acquaintances as they walked around. They saw a few movies and Shatru was amused by Joyce's childlike delight at Peter Seller's antics in *The Mouse That Roared*. Sooner than expected, it was time for his house guests to arrive.

Shatru's closest friend, Abhijeet, the prince of Almara, drove up first. He was not married, like Shatru, and they had grown up together on adjoining estates and had gone to the same school and college. The friends shook hands and walked a little away from the group of servants who were waiting in the hall to receive the guests.

"All okay?" Abhijeet inquired as he lit their cigarettes after offering one to his friend.

"Well, the old coot is coming too," said Shatru.

Abhijeet did not need to be told who the old coot was.

"Hmm. Well, we'll just have to manage. Robert okay?"

"He's fine," said Shatru as they turned back towards the front door.

Her Highness, Geetanjali Rathore, Maharani of Sartajpur, arrived just when the sun was setting. All the other house guests had already arrived. Her Rolls Royce drew up to the front door and Robert was at hand to assist her to alight. Dressed in a figure-hugging chiffon sari, her immaculately coiffured hair and made-up face looked ravishing in the fading light. As a master of effect, perhaps that was the reason why she drew up late. She was not precisely old, but it would be quite a stretch of imagination to call her young.

Walking towards her, Shatru took her hands in his, drew her close and planted a kiss on her cheek. Geetanjali blushed appropriately and looked adoringly at him. Arm in arm, they walked into the hall. Abhijeet and Joyce came forward and shook hands. She patted Abhijeet on his cheek, having known him since he was a boy, and looked Joyce up and down as if she was a particularly noisome slug that she had found in her salad. With that, she strolled to the Garden Suite whose doors were being held open for her by Robert.

"Oh! The Garden Suite! How perfectly lovely," she exclaimed in a musical contralto voice. "The old maharaja used to live here, but how would I possibly know that ..." she tailed off, realising her faux pas. With that, she disappeared to dress for dinner, with her maid at her heels. The others breathed a collective sigh of relief.

"Patsy hasn't shown up yet. He's coming on the day before the party," said Shatru. The two friends were enjoying a pre-pre-dinner aperitif in the library before the house guests came down for the cocktail hour. Patsy was the rather unkind nickname bestowed on the Maharaja of Sartajpur, His Highness Prem Prakash Rathore.

"Well, that should make things easier," said Abhijeet.

"When?" Shatru inquired.

"Tomorrow morning, after breakfast. Take her for a drive or something," said Abhijeet.

Shatru nodded and the two friends got up to join the others in the hall.

After rising fashionably late the next morning, the maharani had a sparse breakfast consisting of dry toast, a boiled egg, and black coffee. Thus restored, she graciously agreed to the drive offered by Shatru and they duly set off on Tehri Road in Shatru's Buick. The rest of the household was left to their own devices, mostly lounging on the circular veranda nourished by copious draughts of the excellent coffee that Robert brought in at regular intervals.

There was a small room adjoining the Garden Suite. It was accessed by an inconspicuous door and in the unlikely event that the door was noticed at all, it seemed to just lead to an ordinary box room. Abhijeet walked in quietly after Shatru and the maharani had left. Once inside, he flicked on the light and opened a small door set in the side wall. It opened into a large, built-in cupboard in the dressing room of the Garden Suite. Very quietly, he went through to find himself amidst many feminine clothes and accessories. The delicate fragrance of jasmine floated in the air. He opened the cupboard door a crack to see if there was anyone around, but the suite was empty after the cleaning maids had done their work.

There was a safe built into the wall of the cupboard. Shatru had given a key to the maharani to keep her valuables, but there was another one that Abhijeet used to open the safe. There were several jewel cases, and a purse stuffed with money. He quickly went through the jewel cases and gave a grunt of disappointment when he did not find what he was looking for. Just when he had finished and was closing the safe, he heard the handle of the front door of the suite opening stealthily. As he was inside the cupboard, he could not be seen, but he quickly made his way back to the small door leading to the box room. He went through it but left the door slightly ajar so that he could see if someone opened the cupboard.

Sure enough, quiet footsteps came up to the cupboard and the door was opened. He could see a feminine hand reach inside and try the lock of the safe. At this point, Abhijeet closed the door and quietly stepped inside the box room. Heaving a silent sigh of relief, he came out of the box room and took his place amongst the loungers on the veranda where coffee had given way to beer as the morning progressed.

"It wasn't there," said Abhijeet. They were seated under the shade of a large deodar tree in the garden after lunch. Most of the guests were snoozing in their rooms after a large lunch accompanied by some excellent Chablis and Riesling from the cellars of Oliver's Castle.

"Yes, I know, she told me that Patsy would be bringing it as he was worried about her security as she was travelling alone," said Shatru with a sigh.

"Damn!" Abhijeet said as he stubbed out his cigarette. "There's another problem. We've got competition."

With that, Abhijeet told his friend about what had happened in the Garden Suite.

"So, it's a woman," said Shatru musingly. "Would you be able to identify her?"

"Well, she's got mighty pretty hands," said Abhijeet with a laugh. "That's all I saw."

"Wonder how she planned to open the safe. If you don't have a key, it would need an experienced cracksman to do it. Maybe she was after the other jewellery or the money. Either way, we should know by tonight after the maharani opens the safe to take out her jewellery to dress for the evening. Damn it to hell. This really fouls things up," said Shatru feelingly.

That evening, the maharani dazzled the party. She was dressed in a deep green sari with her hair up. She was wearing a magnificent emerald necklace, and it was evident that the safe had not been rifled as it would have been one of the first things to go.

"So, it looks like nothing was taken from the safe. Maybe she could not open it," mused Shatru.

"Patsy arrives tomorrow, so that's our last chance. Knowing him, he will leave at the crack of dawn and arrive by ten at the latest."

Abhijeet nodded. "Yes, we'll give it another try tomorrow morning. Let's join the others now."

They drained their glasses and stepped out of the library to see a very lively sing-song and impromptu dancing in progress. Joyce was playing the piano and the maharani was singing the Supremes hit from last year:

"Baby, baby, baby don't leave me
Ooh, please don't leave me all by myself
I've got this burning, burning, yearning feelin' inside me
Ooh, deep inside me and it hurts so bad"

Shatru and Abhijeet joined the fun. After a while, when Joyce stopped playing, they switched to a radiogram and the party continued.

"Well, those two seem to be on the best of terms," said Abhijeet under his breath to Shatru who was standing beside him. Joyce and the maharani were seated on a small sofa and were giggling like schoolgirls. Their glasses of wine were rapidly replenished by the attentive Robert, and it seemed that several refills had already happened. The initial coldness between the two was obviously a thing of the past.

The party wound up quite late. Joyce and the maharani had left earlier. Shatru was already in bed when Joyce came in.

"Well, well, you seem to be as thick as thieves with the maharani," said Shatru as she got into bed and snuggled up to him.

Joyce giggled and said, "She's sweet. A little nutty and quite old, but she's fun! She told me so many things about her life with the old man."

"The old man happens to be one of the richest men in the country," Shatru added dryly.

"Oh well, that hardly matters," said Joyce breathily as she turned her attention towards better things.

Patsy lived up to his reputation. At 9.45 sharp the next morning, his Bentley drove up to Oliver's Castle. Shatru welcomed him at the porch. Patsy was tall and thin and walked with a stoop. He wore gold-rimmed glasses and looked like a professor. His wife embraced him with a slight peck on his cheek before the royal couple went into the Garden Suite for Patsy to bathe and change after his long drive. They emerged soon thereafter and Shatru sat with them for a belated breakfast after which Patsy and

Geetanjali happily accepted his offer for a stroll around the garden to see the flowers that were out in full glory.

Abhijeet saw them leaving and unobtrusively went into the box room. He had opened the safe and was engrossed in looking through the jewellery when the cupboard door opened. He turned quickly and saw that it was Joyce who had opened the door. She had a key to the safe in her hand and it was difficult to see who was more surprised.

Abhijeet recovered first. "So, it was you who had opened the door the other day."

"How do you know?" Joyce said.

"I just do. Let's get out of here before someone else comes in," said Abhijeet. With that, he picked up the famous Jawahar Diamond Necklace with the principal stone weighing in at 37 carats and put it into his pocket. He then took out a replica and placed it carefully in the jewel case. He shut and locked the safe and gestured for Joyce to meet him outside. Then, turning aside, he went back to the box room. As he came out, Joyce joined him, and they went out into the veranda.

"I have a gun in my pocket and I'm not afraid to use it, so keep your mouth shut. We will talk when Shatru comes back," muttered Abhijeet. Joyce nodded. Very soon, the royals returned from their walk and settled down for coffee on the veranda. Shatru made his apologies for the delay, citing work to be done for the party tomorrow, and made his way to his bedroom with the other two following.

"Well?" Shatru asked.

In response, Abhijeet took out the Jawahar Diamond Necklace and placed it on the table.

"She's the one who was trying to open the safe the other day," said Abhijeet, gesturing towards Joyce. "She surprised me while I was opening the safe today. She had a key!"

Shatru turned his attention to Joyce. "It certainly seems that you are much more devious than I gave you credit for. Explain yourself."

"My mother used to work in the Sartajpur Palace. She was an Anglo-Indian and was very beautiful. Her parents had died and had left her in the care of Patsy's father," said Joyce.

"Go on. What has that got to do with this?" Shatru said.

"Patsy's father raped my mother, and she became pregnant. I was the child. He lost interest in my mother after that and sent her to a convent where I was raised by the nuns. That was in Bareilly. My mother died when I was a teenager. She made me swear that I would take revenge for what had happened to her," said Joyce.

"Well, that's pretty melodramatic! Almost like a B-Grade movie," said Abhijeet.

Joyce turned on him fiercely. "Well, whatever I am, I'm not a cheap crook like the two of you."

"Enough of this!" Shatru said commandingly. "How did you get hold of the key of the safe?"

Joyce shrugged her shoulders. "Easy enough. The maharani was quite drunk when we came to her suite. She had hidden the key in a little box that had some trinkets in it. She took it out when she thought I was not looking as I pretended to fall asleep on her bed. I had tried opening the safe earlier with a skeleton key, but it did not work."

Shatru gazed at her with new-found admiration. "My my, you're a clever one, aren't you."

"Still better than a cheap crook, for sure," said Joyce sneeringly.

Shatru sighed. "Tell her," he said, gesturing to Abhijeet. He lit a cigarette and tossed the pack to his friend.

"Have you heard of the Sulochana Foundation?" Abhijeet asked as he lit his own cigarette.

"Yes, of course. They are the ones who run schools in small towns and villages. What does this have to do with that?" Joyce asked.

"Everything," said Shatru. "We *are* the Sulochana Foundation. Sulochana was my mother's name. Robert is the only one other than us who knows about what we do. We started the operation a few years ago and went begging for money from these plutocrats. They were not willing to donate a penny. Most of them have shady pasts like our dear Patsy who has made his money by growing opium on his estate illegally. We just decided to help them to become a little more generous."

"The modus operandi is quite simple. We had good quality duplicates made of expensive and well-known pieces of jewellery and substituted them for the originals. The Garden Party is a big draw for the rich and famous, so we've had a good strike rate over the years. The best part is that since these jewels are largely bought from ill-gotten money, the owners are understandably reluctant to go to the police even if they find out that the jewels are not real. So far, there have been no complaints," said Abhijeet with a laugh.

"Well, now you know all about us, so?" Shatru said.

Joyce had been listening intently as the friends spoke in tandem. After a long pause, she said, "Perhaps you need another partner. Would I do?"

Shatru looked at Abhijeet, who nodded. "Well, you've got yourself a deal," he said laughingly.

"So now there are three of us!" Joyce exclaimed. She shook hands with both friends, and then together they started moving towards the door to be with their forgotten guests. Shatru put his arm around Joyce's waist and pulled her close.

"Two-plus-one would be a more accurate representation," drawled Abhijeet as he winked at his lifelong friend.

Acknowledgements

The idea of an eclectic collection of short stories about Mussoorie had been brewing in my mind for a long time. Like all hill stations, Mussoorie too has a long history of itinerant summer visitors while permanent residents are relatively few. The sense of community is therefore different from a settled township where people know their neighbours well. This adds a unique piquancy and inquisitiveness to social interaction. The diverse range of summer visitors also makes for an interesting potpourri of attitudes, experiences, secrets, and social classes. This diversity lies at the heart of the vivid montage that Mussoorie society displayed in the 1960s and '70s when Indian hill stations were thriving.

I have read these stories out aloud to my sister, Jyotsna Raj, who is a discerning and constructive critic of all my writing. Her eager anticipation for the next instalment over a week spent at Ida Villa, our house in Mussoorie, was reward enough for the hard work involved in the writing of this book. My daughters, Priya and Anuradha, have loved these stories, though they were not born in the era that is depicted here. The encouragement from my wife, Devi, my friends Shashi Kalathil, Kishore and Nirja Asthana, Ashok and Nalini Swarup, and a host of others from my class at IIM Calcutta, who have read some of these stories has been a great source of satisfaction for me.

I would like to thank Ajay Mago of Om Books International for consistently believing in my work. Shantanu Ray Chaudhuri, editor-in-chief, Om Books International, decided to publish these stories even before my first book with Om, *The Mussoorie Murders*, had seen the light of day. Shantanu also suggested the title for this collection, so his support has been invaluable. Sakschi Verma, my editor, has contributed in no small measure to the volume that is in your hands today.

My brilliant literary agent, Suhail Mathur, CEO of The Book Bakers, has played a major part in my literary journey.

I hope you will enjoy your tryst with old Mussoorie. There is something about these hills that calls you back again and again. For old addicts like me, nothing gives me more pleasure than seeing new devotees joining the cause.